W9-BCY-801

# IROQUOIS

Michael G. Johnson

# IROQUOIS
## People of the Longhouse

# FIREFLY BOOKS

# A FIREFLY BOOK

Published by Firefly Books Ltd. 2013

First printing

**Publisher Cataloging-in-Publication Data (U.S.)**
Johnson, Michael G.
Iroquois : people of the longhouse / Michael G. Johnson.
[160] p. : col. ill., col. photos., maps ;   cm.
Includes bibliographical references and index.
Chapters include: history, culture, material culture, people and gazetteer.
ISBN-13: 978-1-77085-218-1
1. Iroquoian Indians.  2. Iroquois Indians – Social life and customs.
3. Iroquois Indians – Politics and government.  4. Iroquois art.  I.
Title
970.00497 dc23    E99.I7J6457 2013

**Library and Archives Canada Cataloguing in Publication**
Johnson, Michael G., author
Iroquois : people of the longhouse / Michael G. Johnson.
Includes bibliographical references and index.
ISBN 978-1-77085-218-1 (bound)
1. Iroquois Indians--History.  2. Iroquois Indians--Social
life and customs.  I. Title.
E99.I7J64 2013    970.004'9755    C2013-903202-9

Published in the United States by
Firefly Books (U.S.) Inc.
P.O. Box 1338, Ellicott Station
Buffalo, New York 14205

Published in Canada by
Firefly Books Ltd.
50 Staples Avenue, Unit 1
Richmond Hill, Ontario L4B 0A7

Designed by Greene Media Ltd

Printed in China

In memory
of Sarah

**Acknowledgments and credits**

The author would like to thank the following for their help with comments, suggestions, photographs, but any omissions and errors are the author's alone: Jack Heriard, Whispering Wind Magazine, LA; Frank Bergevin, Alexandria Bay, NY; Yvonne Thomas (Six Nations), ON; Gerry Biron, Saxtons River, VT; Arthur Einhorn, Loweville, NY; Jack Hayes (deceased), Lands End, UK; Cath Oberholzter, Cobourg, ON; Timothy O'Sullivan, Stourbridge, UK; Rob Hunter, UK.

Unless specified below, all photographs were taken by the Author or from the Author's Collection. All maps and diagrams by Mark Franklin. Artwork on pages 78–80 by Jonathan Smith (contact jonathanpsmith59@yahoo.co.uk for purchase of original work). Thanks to Simon Clay for photography of Author's Collection.

1 Simon Clay; 2 Written Heritage Collection; 7 and 8 The Art Archive/Musée du Nouveau Monde La Rochelle/Gianni Dagli Orti; 12B Library of Congress Prints & Photographs Division, Washington, D.C. 20540 (henceforth LoCP&P) Bain Collection; 13BR Gerry Biron; 14 (both) Simon Clay; 16–17 Library of Congress Geography and Map Division Washington D.C. 20540-4650 (henceforth LoCG&M); 19 inset Library and Archives of Canada; 25 LoCP&P; 26 Library and Archives of Canada, Acc No. 1977-35-3 Acquired with a special grant from the Canadian Government in 1977; 27 Wikipedia; 31 LoCG&M; 34L British Museum; 34R Wikipedia; 35 LoCP&P; 36 Library and Archives of Canada; 38L Gerry Biron; 39 LoCG&M; 41T Library and Archives of Canada; 47 Library and Archives of Canada, Acc No. 1977-35-1 Acquired with a special grant from the Canadian Government in 1977; 48A Getty Images 51246190; 50T Library and Archives of Canada; 50BL, 50BR, and 51 Written Heritage Collection; 52 Marilyn Angel Wynn/Getty Images 77061854; 53T Written Heritage Collection; 53B and 54–55B Library and Archives of Canada; 58B Simon Clay; 62–63B American School/Getty Images 147852618; 66–67T Library and Archives of Canada; 66B and 67B Frank Bergevin Collection; 68, 69, and 70 Simon Clay; 71T Frank Bergevin Collection; 72T Marilyn Angel Wynn/Getty Images 88642473; 72B Nativestock.com/ Marilyn Angel Wynn/Getty Images 150394812; 73T Lee Snider/Photo Images/Corbis SN005187; 73B Getty Images 143231511; 76 Copy of a tintype by Gerry Biron; 81 inset Frank Bergenin and Naomi Smith; 84L Gerry Biron; 85L Written Heritage Collection; 85TL Gerry Biron; 86B Royal Albert Memorial Museum, Exeter, UK; 87BL and R Frank Bergevin; 92TL Electric Studio/Library and Archives Canada/C-085137; 92R Richard Hamell; 94–95BR, BTMR, and TR Richard D. Hamell; 98TL Author's sketches of masks in Museum of the American Indian Heye Foundation now the National Museum of the American Indian; 100 Helmet Weber; 106 Frank Bergevin and Yvonne Thomas; 107 Jake Thomas Learning Center, Six Nations Reserve, Ontario; 111BL & BR Frank Bergevin; 115 Frank Bergevin; 116 & 117 Gerry Biron; 118T Gerry Biron; 118B Frank Bergevin Collection; 120–121 Gerry Biron except 120B Frank Bergevin Collection; 122 & 123TR & BR Frank Bergevin Collection; 125L both Simon Clay; 125BR Schoharie Museum of the Iroquois Indian, Schoharie, NY; 126B, 127–129 Simon Clay; 130T, 131T & BR, 132–133 Frank Bergevin Collection; 134–135 Simon Clay; 136 Written Heritage Collection; 137 Library and Archives of Canada, Acc No. 1977-35-2 Acquired with a special grant from the Canadian Government in 1977; 138 From lithographs in McKenney and Hall's, The Indian Tribes of North America, Vols. I & II, John Grant Edinburgh, 1933–1934; 139 Library and Archives of Canada, Acc No. 1977-35-4 Acquired with a special grant from the Canadian Government in 1977; 140T LoCP&P; 141T Dominion of Canada Rifle Association/ Library and Archives Canada/PA-134828; LoCP&P; 142T Getty Images 113625134; 142B From a lithographs in McKenney and Hall; 143B LoCP&P; 144T Getty Images 51242541; 144B Getty Images 3087696; 145T Library and Archives Canada, Acc. No. 1984-119-1; 145B LoCP&P; 148TL Cephas via WikiCommons; 148B LoCP&P; 149T LoCG&M; 150T LoCP&P HABS NwY,29-FORJO,1-7 (Thos. T. Waterman photographer); 150C Photographs in the Carol M. Highsmith Archive, LoCP&P; 152T LoCP&P HABS NY, 18-JONTO, 1-10 (Nelson E. Baldwin photographer); 152C HABS NY, 18-JONTO, 1A-1 (Stanley P. Mixon photographer).

Captions: Page 1 See page 126; Page 2 Jim Longfeather, Seneca, wearing a beaded jacket and headband, c. 1901.

# Contents

# Introduction

## THE ORIGINS OF THE IROQUOIS CONFEDERACY

The date of the unification of five linguistically related but separate tribes who lived along the rivers and lakeshores in what is now northern New York State is unknown. Native tradition puts the date long before the arrival of Europeans in the early 16th century, but evidence suggests a likely date of around the middle of the 1500s, perhaps even in response to this threatening event. The Confederacy is called Haudenosaunee — People of the Longhouse — by themselves. The French called them *Les Iroquois* and the British later called them the Five Nations. We know of the founding of the Confederacy from the so-called "Deganawida Epic" even though each narrator has his own version of the myth. However, the main details can be outlined thus.

Deganawida was probably born on the north shore of Lake Ontario, possibly a Huron. He brought a message of peace, righteousness, and civil authority to the Mohawks. Among them he met Ayouhwatha, glossed Hiawatha (subsequently transformed by the poet Longfellow into an Ojibwa), a troubled chief who had lost children in violent circumstances, whom he condoled. Together Deganawida and Ayouhwatha visited all the five tribes who were subsequently induced to form the Confederacy, although they met resistance from the Onondaga sorcerer Thadodaho, who — after he reformed — became one of the 50 founding Confederacy Chiefs drawn from all the village chiefs of the five tribes. Metaphors of union included the planting of the Tree of Peace, a magnificent white pine beneath which representatives of the Five Nations buried their weapons of war, and from the tree four long roots — "White Roots of Peace" — extended in the cardinal directions. Deganawida, the Peacemaker, proclaimed that other tribes would be welcomed beneath the tree provided they followed the laws of the Great Peace (or Great Law). Metaphors of union applied equally to local families, village, tribe, and Confederacy. The 50 Confederacy Chiefs (Peace Chiefs) had emblems of identity, including their title names, which were passed on to their chosen successors in each generation until today. Council speakers employed (and still do) mnemonic devices to "prop up their minds" to record historical and political events with wampum belts with appropriate designs or condolence canes that carried carved designs to recall titles of the 50 founders of the League. However, many pre-unification leaders were warriors so that after unification there was a distinction between the Peace Chiefs and the Pine Tree Chiefs, the latter being warriors. This method of honoring warriors

ensured that their ambitions would be satisfied without danger of overthrowing the League's constitution.

The Confederated five tribes were, from east to west, the Mohawk, Oneida, Onondaga, Cayuga, and Seneca. They occupied a land of forest and lakes from the Mohawk River to the Genesee. Collectively, they likened this domain to a huge longhouse where the Mohawks were "Keepers of the Eastern Door," the Seneca "Keepers of the Western Door," and the centrally located Onondaga "Keepers of the Great Fire," their main village often considered the capital of the nation. Old theories suggesting that the migration of the Iroquoian peoples took place from the Ohio Valley or from the south have been now largely discarded and archaeological evidence suggests the Iroquois genesis was within their area of historic occupation and linked to cultural phases around Lake Simcoe, Ontario, below Montreal on the St. Lawrence, central New York and along the Susquehanna River. Linguistic studies reveal the five tribes spoke related but not mutually intelligible languages and were further related to a dozen other languages that constitute the Iroquoian linguistic family, which can be arranged dialectically as follows:

**The Iroquoian Language Family**

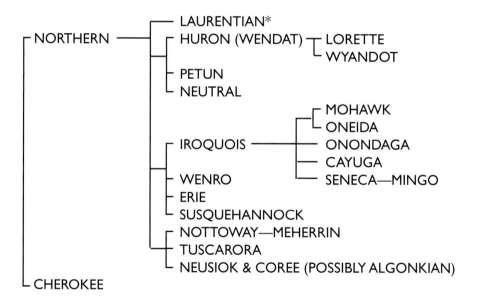

The Huron (or Wendat) were also in a confederation about Lake Simcoe and Georgian Bay, Ontario. The Petun, otherwise known as the Tobacco Nation (Tionontati), lived close to the Huron on Nottawasaga Bay; the Neutral between the Grand and Niagara rivers, with a closely related people — the Wenro — just across the border in present day New York State. The Erie, Nation of the Cat or Raccoon, were along the southern shore of Lake Erie. These peoples, who were not part of the Iroquois Confederacy, were overrun and dispersed by the middle of the 17th century as the Iroquois expanded in search of new hunting grounds for beaver fur as much of their own territory had already been trapped out in trade with the French and Dutch eager for peltry (pelts). Some of these peoples were absorbed by the Iroquois, others subsequently reformed and became the Wyandot or lived under French protection —such as the Hurons at Lorette near Quebec.

It was always a question of "those who are not with us are against us," despite

**Opposite:** Woman carrying a child on her back, possibly Mohawk, of the 18th century. Her attire, except for the moccasins, is entirely of European trade material. She wears a cloth blanket and red cloth leggings with silver earrings. The child is carried by means of a burden strap across the forehead (probably in a cradleboard). Watercolor, by an unknown artist.

*Laurentian is a linguistic term for an Iroquoian language recorded by Cartier's expeditions 1534–1535, spoken near modern Montreal. Nothing more is known of the language or the people who spoke it.

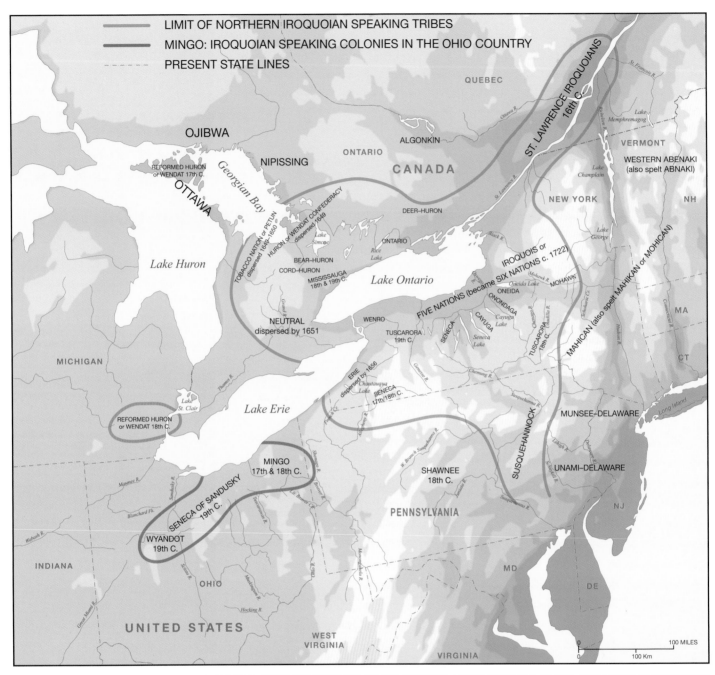

LIMIT OF NORTHERN IROQUOIAN SPEAKING TRIBES

MINGO: IROQUOIAN SPEAKING COLONIES IN THE OHIO COUNTRY

PRESENT STATE LINES

**Right:** Battle between the French and their Algonkian allies and Mohawks along the shore of Lake Champlain in 1609. De Champlain stands in front of his Iroquois enemies with his "hurler of thunder."

**Opposite:** Iroquois statue at the memorial to John Graves Simcoe (1752–1806), first British governor of Upper Canada 1791–1796, in Exeter Cathedral, England.

the peaceful arrangements at the foundation of the League. The Susquehannock (or Conestoga) of Pennsylvania, living in the valley of the Susquehanna River, were friends of the Hurons. After the loss of their Huron allies they made an alliance with the Maryland colonists in 1661, who subsequently made peace with the Senecas and then turned against their former allies. The Susquehannocks, like the Hurons, Petuns, Neutrals, and Eries were dispersed, the last of them were living at Conestoga (near present day Lancaster) with Iroquois sanction, and were murdered by white "Indian haters" from Pantang in 1763.

The Nottoway and Meherrin were small groups in Southern Virginia and the Tuscaroras lived along the rivers flowing east into Pamlico Sound. Following a savage war with the North Carolina colonists, the Tuscaroras requested to live among the Iroquois. None of the Nottoway and Meherrin — although likely Iroquoian and related to the Tuscarora — as far as is known, moved north to join the Iroquois. However, moving north the majority of the Tuscaroras were adopted as members of the League in 1722 — the Five Nations thus becoming the Six Nations — and they became near equal partners. At the Albany Treaty of 1722 the Iroquois were reluctantly required by the colonial governors to police various small groups of Pennsylvania Indians, some of whom were ultimately absorbed into the Confederacy. Those tribes, small in numbers, protected by the Iroquois were known as the "Props of the Iroquois."

The most divergent Iroquois language was that of the Cherokee, the largest tribe of the whole language family who occupied a great area in the southern Appalachian Mountains, a region floristically similar to the plateau of central-north New York State homeland of the Iroquois. Although there were superficial similarities in culture between the Cherokee and Iroquois, the language difference suggests a separation from a parent tongue of perhaps 2,000 years. In 1534 and 1535 Jacques Cartier made the first known European contacts with people along the St. Lawrence River widely believed to be Iroquoian, now called Laurentian, but their relationship to any known later Iroquois tribe is not known.

## THE SIX NATIONS

### MOHAWK

The most easterly tribe of the Iroquois Confederacy, their name was derived from the Algonkian "Man Eaters," but in their own language they were Ganienkeh, "People of the Place of the Flint." Their location at the time of contact with Europeans was the Mohawk River area of present day New York State. In 1609 they were in a skirmish with the French under Champlain near the lake which bears his name.

Wars with the Dutch and Mohicans in 1624 were followed by the Indian-White alliances ultimately known as the "Covenant Chain," first in 1643 and later in 1677 at Albany. The Mohawks at first resisted French missionaries, putting to death Fr. Isaac Jogues, but later during breaks in the fighting with the French about one third of the Mohawks withdrew to the Catholic missions in French Canada and from then on were their allies until the surrender of Canada in 1760. During the 18th century the remaining Mohawks in their old country became particularly friendly with the British under Sir William Johnson, who dealt through them to manipulate the Six Nations in their interest. They fought with the British during the French and Indian War and American Revolution but following the British defeat were led to Upper Canada by Joseph Brant, their leader. Their descendants today are at Six Nations, Tyendinaga, and Gibson in Ontario; in Quebec Oka (Kanehsatake), Caughnawaga (Kahnawake), and St. Regis (Akwesasne) at the junction of Quebec, Ontario, and New York states; and at

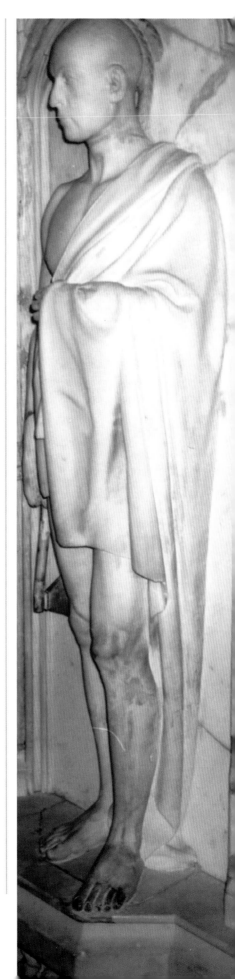

**Above:** Hodjiga De (William Fish Carrier), 1901. A Cayuga chief from the Six Nations Reserve, Ontario, Canada, photographed by DeLancy Gill while visiting the Smithsonian Institution, Washington DC.

**Right:** Two Wampum belts, the Onondaga Alliance Belt (above) commemorating the coming of Tuscaroras in 1713, and the Wolf Treaty Belt (below) representing the alliance of the Mohawks with the French. The wolves symbolize the "Door Keepers" of the League.

two recently formed communities in New York, Ganienkeh and Kanatsioharee. A few Mohawk fur traders found their way to Alberta (the Michel Band) mixed with Crees, but were enfranchised in 1958. In 1890, 6,980 Mohawks were estimated exclusive of the Alberta band.

## ONEIDA

"People of the Erect (Standing) Stone," they lived around the creek and lake that bears their name in New York State. During the American Revolution they sided with the Americans along with the Tuscaroras, following which, many moved to live with the Onondagas, their own lands reduced to but a few acres. Under the influence of Eleazar Williams, the Mohawk minister, many Oneidas moved to Wisconsin in the 1830s and others under the leadership of Moses Schuyler and William Doxtator moved to the Thames River, Ontario in 1840. Their communities today are the Oneida Reservation, Wisconsin; Oneidatown and Six Nations, Ontario and the small but growing Oneida Reservation, New York, although relatively few actually still live on these reserves. The small Oneida reservation in Madison County, NY, now boasts the highly successful Turning Stone Casino, several business ventures, and a tribal museum reflecting the huge changes that have recently taken place.

## ONONDAGA

"People of the Hill," their main village, Onondaga Castle, although it moved several times was considered the capital of the Iroquois Confederacy. As "Keepers of the Central (Great) Fire" they were charged with the responsibility of convening its councils. They lived around Skaneateles and Cazenovia Lakes and on Onondaga Creek. They were divided by the American Revolution, after which some moved with the British Loyalists to Six Nations, Ontario, while the remainder drifted back to old Onondaga south of modern Syracuse where their descendants remain. Important wampum belts have recently been returned to them as important records of old treaties.

## CAYUGA

Their name is of unknown origin possibly meaning "People of the Great Swamp." They lived between Cayuga and Owasco Lakes in upper New York. At the close of the American Revolution, following their association with the British, they mostly withdrew to Upper Canada with Brant's Mohawks; the last of their tribal lands in New York were sold in 1841. Those remaining, a group of mixed Senecas and Cayugas, found their way to Oklahoma where a mixed blood group still remains. A few incorporated with the

Senecas at the Cattaraugus Reservation, NY. Recently a few acres of land at Seneca Falls in their old territory have been purchased by Cayuga people.

## SENECA

Probably an Algonkian corruption, their name means "Great Hills People," and they kept watch over the "Western Door" of the Confederacy. They lived along the Genesee River to Canandaigua Lake and were possibly the largest tribe at the foundation of the League. Their lands were invaded by Generals Sullivan and Clinton during the American Revolution, their crops and villages destroyed. Although some moved to Canada after the war, many remained in New York and in spite of fraudulent transactions with land companies in 1826 and 1838 that saw the sale of their lands in western New York, they managed to regain reservations at Allegany, Cattaraugus, and Tonawanda. A small group accompanied the Cayuga to Oklahoma: the Senecas of Sandusky, descendants of Senecas in the Ohio country.

The total population of the original Five Nations has been given as low as 10,000 and as high as 20,000 between 1500 to 1650, split fairly evenly among the tribes with perhaps the Senecas and Mohawks slightly more numerous than the others. Today the total Iroquois enrolled and registered membership is in excess of 90,000 (of which approximately 60,000 are in Canada) but almost totally mixed racially and tribally.

**Below left:** Robert David (Gadji Nenda He), Cayuga, Six Nations Reserve, Ontario. He holds an iron (probably) pipe-tomahawk and wears metal brooches and a fur turban. Photographed by DeLancy Gill while visiting the Smithsonian Institution, Washington, DC in 1903.

**Below:** Goldie Jamison Conklin (c. 1891–1974). A Seneca of the Heron Clan, Allegany Reservation, NY. Note the beaded headdress, moccasins, and pouch.

**Below:** Both sides of an Iroquois beaded bag, from c.1880. This example is inscribed "From Niagara Falls," is 3.5 inches (8.8 cm) square, and constructed with stiffened fabric, cotton-tape edging, and decorated with clear glass beads. This type of souvenir bag was probably the work of the Tuscarora Indians whose reservation is close to the famous Falls.

## TUSCARORA

The name probably means "Hemp Shirt Wearers." The Tuscarora spoke a language of the Iroquoian stock and lived along the rivers flowing into Pamlico Sound, NC. John Lawson, an early explorer, knew them intimately and described them as mild and friendly but they were victims of kidnapping raids for slaves. The Tuscarora turned savagely on the whites in the so-called Tuscarora War (1711–1713) until their main village, Narhantes, in Greene County, NC, had been destroyed by whites. As a result of this war they requested to "shelter themselves among the Five Nations." Consequently, many Tuscarora journeyed north and were admitted into the Iroquois as a Sixth Nation by 1722. However, it was 90 years before their migration from the south was complete and their passage through Pennsylvania is still marked by numerous place names. At the close of the American Revolution some moved to the Six Nations Reserve, Ontario, and the remainder obtained a reserve near Niagara Falls. They became well known for the production of Indian arts and crafts sold to visitors to the Falls in the 19th century and became almost totally acculturated. In 1990, 664 Tuscarora were reported in New York and 1,926 in Ontario in 2005. Today there are few native speakers of their language. A few Tuscarora are said to have not made the journey north and may have descendants among the mixed-descent groups of North Carolina. One estimate puts their population at about 5,000 in 1600.

## INCORPORATED AND ASSOCIATED TRIBES — THE "PROPS OF THE LONGHOUSE"

### NANTICOKE

The Nanticoke were an Algonkian people who lived in villages along the eastern shore of Maryland and along the Nanticoke River. About 1680, after the Iroquois had gained military control over the Susquehannocks, they became "tributary" to the Iroquois, accepting protection. With increased friction between the Nanticoke and the whites, they requested permission to move into Pennsylvania in 1742 under the Confederacy's protection. They continued to move north and by 1753 were at Chenango the "Southern Door of the Longhouse." At a conference in 1753 and at Johnson Hall in 1766 the chiefs of the Six Nations formally adopted the Nanticokes and a few Conoys and accorded two chiefs to represent them at meetings of the council at Onondaga. However not all (as with the Tuscarora) moved north: a number still remain in Sussex County, DE. Those among the Iroquois found their way to Six Nations Reserve, Ontario, but are no longer separately reported.

### TUTELO

The Tutelo were a small Siouan tribe who lived in the Piedmont region of Virginia and North Carolina. The Susquehannocks attempted to disperse the Tutelos after they, in turn, had been pushed south by the Iroquois in 1675. To protect themselves the Tutelo moved into the mountains at the headwaters of the Yadkin River, then east to the Meherrin. Having made peace with the Iroquois in 1722 they moved north to Pennsylvania where Conrad Weiser found them in 1744 at Shamokin. They were adopted as "Younger Brothers" of the Iroquois in 1753, ultimately merged with the Cayugas and moved with them to the Six Nations Reserve, Canada. The Cayugas at

**Left:** Mohawks from Caughnawaga (Kahnawaka) Reserve near Montreal, c. 1900. The man wears a buckskin jacket and beaded collar. The Mohawks were partly won over to French interests in the 17th century while others remained allies of the British until the American Revolution, after which they, too, moved largely to Canada.

**Above:** Solomon O'Bail (1814–1899), c. 1860. A Seneca, he was the grandson of the famous Cornplanter. He wears a large Iroquois-style bandolier bag.

Six Nations continued to conduct an annual Tutelo Spirit Adoption Ceremony into the 20th century, although there were no Tutelo-speaking people remaining. However, a text recorded from their few remaining descendants in the late 19th century confirmed their language as probably Siouan.

## MINGO

Mingo is a term for detached Iroquois bands or villages in the Ohio Country, an area often claimed as hunting grounds, these villages were usually Seneca but probably incorporated remnants of tribes destroyed by the Iroquois in the 17th century, and fragments of other tribes such as Wyandot, Delaware, Ottawa, and Mahican. In the early 19th century they became known as Seneca of Sandusky and accompanied some Cayugas from New York to Indian Territory, where several hundred descendants remain. In the 18th century they were, more often than not, allies of the French.

## THE SEVEN NATIONS OF CANADA

During the breaks in the colonial conflicts between France and Great Britain, perhaps one third of the Mohawks and some Onondagas and Oneidas were won over to French interests and moved to the Catholic missions on or near the St. Lawrence at Caughnawaga, Oka, St. Regis, Oswegatchie (later abandoned). Together with the Abenaki (St. Francis and Becancour) and Huron (Lorette) they formed the "French Indians" or Onontioga.

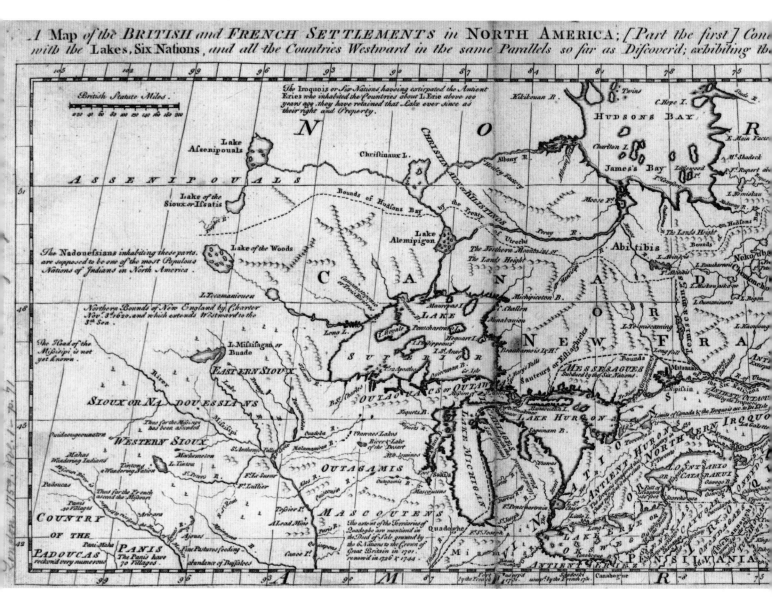

## NEW ENGLAND ALGONKIANS

Upon the invitation of the Oneidas in 1785 the Mahicans (Mohicans) from Stockbridge, MA built a village named New Stockbridge in the Oneida territory. They were followed in 1788 by refugees from southern New England (Mohegan, Pequot, Narragansett, and Montauk) who settled at Brothertown. However, the majority moved on to Wisconsin during the 19th century together with the Oneida to lands acquired from the Menomini Indians.

## THE SIX NATIONS AT GRAND RIVER, ONTARIO, CANADA

To give an indication of the tribal diversity at the Six Nations Reserve, Canada after the settlement following the defeat of the British and their Loyalist Iroquois, a total of 1,843 were reported in 1784–1785. Besides the six Iroquois tribes there were reported 55 Upper Tutelos, 19 Lower Tutelos, 11 Nanticokes, two parties of Delawares of 48 and 183, and 53 Creeks and Cherokees in the population. In 1847 the Six Nations allowed the Mississaugas of Credit to settle in the southwestern corner of the reserve. Their descendants still remain autonomous and numbered 546 in 1970.

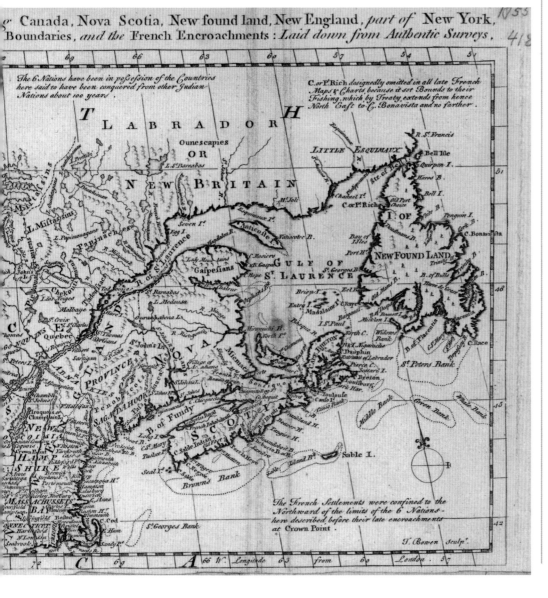

A map of the British and French settlements in North America, indicating Indian tribes and with various mentions of the Iroquois: "The Six Nations have been in possession of the countries said to have been conquered from other Indian Nations about 100 years." It was published in London in 1755.

# Chapter 1: History

**Above:** A 17th century representation of an Iroquois warrior. Note the wooden shield reported by early explorers.

**Opposite:** Fierce Iroquois warriors with tomahawk (pipe-tomahawk in main image), ball-headed club, earrings, facial tattoos, leggings, moccasins, and snow shoes. Two engravings by J. Laroque after drawings by J. Grasset de St. Sauveur in 1787.

## 1500–1750

The first known contact between Europeans and people of Iroquoian lineage took place in July 1534 when the French explorer Jacques Cartier met a fishing party of 300 who had descended the St. Lawrence River to Gaspe. The following year Cartier pushed upriver for short visits to Iroquoian villages, one of which—Hochelaga—was situated on Montreal Island. Several Indians were kidnapped and taken to France, some never to return, as a result of Cartier's voyages between 1534 and 1542. However these "Laurentian Iroquois" had vacated the St. Lawrence region by the time Champlain established the first permanent French base at Quebec in 1608. The following summer he led a military expedition south along the Richelieu River and across the lake which now bears his name. Near the southern end of the lake in July 1609, the French and their Indian allies defeated a party of Mohawks, killing perhaps 50 and taking prisoners. As a result of this encounter—and another in June 1610—a long era of hostility between the French and the Iroquois League ensued, punctuated with periods of truce.

During the first half of the 17th century the Iroquois became almost totally involved in the fur trade. So great was the demand for peltries (pelts) by the Dutch, based at Fort Orange (established 1623) on the Hudson River, and the French in Canada, that by 1640 scarcely a beaver was to be found between the Hudson and the Genesee. This period was punctuated by a series of trade treaties made between the Iroquois and the Europeans. On several occasions, the tribes did not act as a corporate whole (which was not required under Confederacy law). One or more members of the League made separate alliances with the Dutch and their Mahican allies and the French between 1624 and 1645. The Iroquois' demand for European trade goods initiated intensive hunting, and to avoid economic collapse the Iroquois embarked on expansion for additional hunting grounds and to capture the position of middlemen in the fur trade. Thus began the "Beaver Wars" and a series of devastating attacks on their neighbors: both Algonkian and related Iroquoian nations who were trading directly with the French. In rapid succession they attacked the Hurons and Petuns 1649–1650, the Neutrals in 1650–1651, and the Eries 1654–1656. The Hurons, once numerically superior to the Iroquois, were forced to scatter west or seek refuge in French Canada, and some were actually absorbed into the Iroquois.

The French had success in their missionary endeavors among the Hurons on the shores of Georgian Bay where Jesuits had succeeded the Franciscan Recollects in 1639,

18

Huron Longhouse and village c. 1630, reconstruction at Midland, Ontario, photographed 2000. The bark lodge, palisades and platforms of the Iroquois would have been very similar.

although their venture survived only 10 years before invading Iroquois laid waste to much of the country. Huron survivors killed their priests, Jean de Brébeuf and Gabriel Lalemant, in 1649 blaming them for their misfortune. They were subsequently canonized in 1930 along with six others, the North American Martyrs: René Goupil, killed after capture by the Iroquois in 1642; Isaac Jogues and Jean de La Lande, who had been killed in 1646 in the Mohawk villages after a second mission to seek their conversion; Antoine Daniel, killed by the Iroquois at Teanaostaye in July 1648; Charles Garnier, also killed by Iroquois in late 1649; and Noël Chabanel, killed by a Huron in 1649.

The long era of hostility between the Iroquois League and the French had periods of truce during which French missionaries had some success among the Onondagas in 1654–1658 and in the Mohawk country 1667–1687. Ultimately this resulted in the establishment of three permanent Iroquois settlements in French Canada at Oka, Caughnawaga, and St. Regis, and a temporary one at Oswegatchie. These, in turn, formed the basis of a new tribal grouping known as the Seven Nations of Canada. The Mohawk, Oneida, and Onondaga converts who took up residence near the French settlements were expelled from the League thenceforth, but probably accounted for approximately one third of their tribal populations.

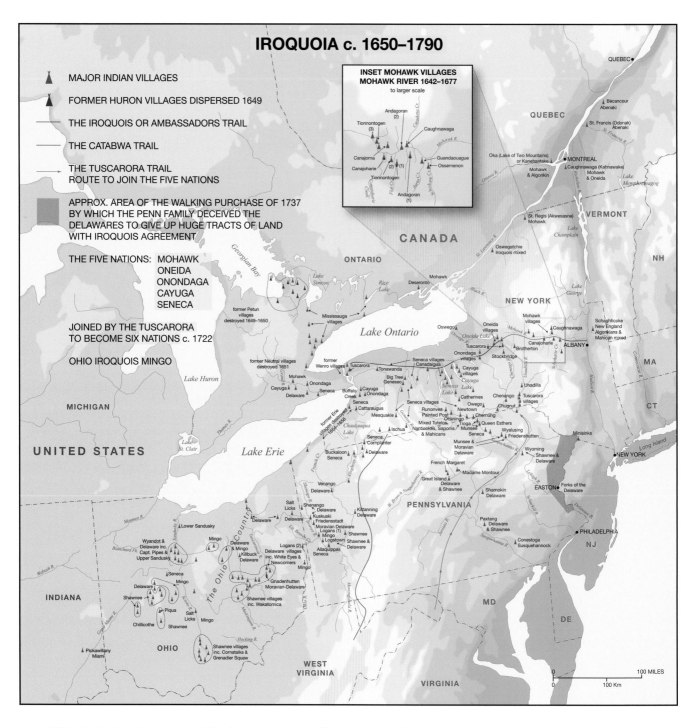

## IROQUOIA c. 1650–1790

**MAJOR INDIAN VILLAGES**

**FORMER HURON VILLAGES DISPERSED 1649**

**THE IROQUOIS OR AMBASSADORS TRAIL**

**THE CATABWA TRAIL**

**THE TUSCARORA TRAIL**
**ROUTE TO JOIN THE FIVE NATIONS**

**APPROX. AREA OF THE WALKING PURCHASE OF 1737 BY WHICH THE PENN FAMILY DECEIVED THE DELAWARES TO GIVE UP HUGE TRACTS OF LAND WITH IROQUOIS AGREEMENT**

**THE FIVE NATIONS: MOHAWK
ONEIDA
ONONDAGA
CAYUGA
SENECA**

**JOINED BY THE TUSCARORA
TO BECOME SIX NATIONS c. 1722**

**OHIO IROQUOIS MINGO**

**INSET MOHAWK VILLAGES
MOHAWK RIVER 1642–1677**
to larger scale

Iroquoia, c. 1650–1790, showing major Indian villages. Note the red Tuscarora Trail, showing the movement of the people northward after the Tuscarora War to join the Five Nations.

The Iroquois met stiffer resistance from the Mahican (popularly known as Mohican) to the east and Susquehannocks to the south. As early as 1626 the Mahicans of the Hudson River valley had driven the Mohawks from their Lower Castle (as the Dutch called the pallisaded village on the Mohawk River east of Schoharie Creek). The Mohawks and Dutch concluded peace agreements between 1643 and 1660 in the metaphor of an "Iron Chain" which was transferred to the English as the Covenant Chain after a treaty at Albany in 1667 following the surrender of New Netherland to the English and the founding of New York in 1664. The last great battle in the war against the Mahican was in 1669 at Hoffman's Ferry, in which the Mohawks were victorious, and peace was concluded in 1673.

After the loss of their Huron allies, the Susquehannocks on the lower Susquehanna River were forced into an alliance with the English settlers in Maryland in 1661. The Senecas launched an attack on the Susquehannocks with 800 warriors in 1663 but were easily repulsed. However, in 1674 the Maryland colonists made a separate peace treaty with the Senecas and declared war on their former allies. The Susquehannocks, like the Hurons, Neutrals, and Eries, were dispersed, some going south, others were adopted by the Iroquois, and a few remnants settled at Conestoga near Lancaster, PA.

In 1666, New France, in order to punish the Iroquois for their raids, launched two military expeditions against the Confederacy. The first, under Sieur de Courcelle, was a failure, but the second, under the new governor, the Marquis de Tracy, burned villages and destroyed corn stores. As a result the Oneidas and Onondagas, with some Cayugas and Senecas, made a peace treaty with the French. The Mohawks, however, remained loyal to the English. The French retaliated by sending a strong force against Mohawks forcing them to sue for peace and to allow the return of the "black-robes" (Jesuit priests) and missions to their villages—and encouraging a further exodus to Canada.

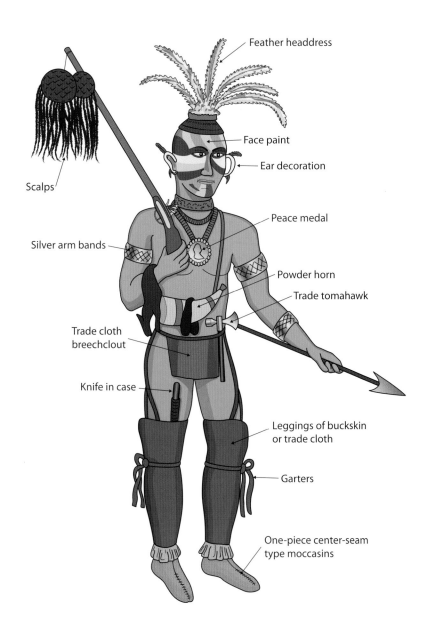

Feather headdress

Face paint

Ear decoration

Scalps

Peace medal

Silver arm bands

Powder horn

Trade tomahawk

Trade cloth breechclout

Knife in case

Leggings of buckskin or trade cloth

Garters

One-piece center-seam type moccasins

An 18th century warrior from the eastern Great Lakes region, based on a contemporary drawing.

**Opposite**: King Hendrick. Recently scholarly re-examination of the life and times of King Hendrick suggests in fact there were two Mohawk chiefs known to the British as Hendrick, or Dutch Peters, whose overlapping lives have been confused into one. The first (c. 1660–1735), a member of the Wolf Clan based at the Lower Castle village, and one of the Four Kings who visited London in 1710, painted by Verelst and presented to Queen Anne. The second, a Mohawk chief of the Bear Clan who lived at the Mohawk Upper Castle village, born c. 1691 and firm friend of Sir William Johnson.

It was he who was killed at the Battle of Lake George in 1755. This is probably the Hendrick illustrated in a contemporary etching, possibly done in London c. 1740; possibly after a painting by an itinerant painter in America.

In 1687 the fragile peace was broken by Marquis de Denonville's invasion of Seneca country with 3,000 men, which destroyed vast quantities of corn. In reprisal, 2 years later Iroquois warriors penetrated New France to the gates of Montreal, devastating the country and killing their crop producers, the so-called Massacre of Lachine. In 1693 and 1696, under Count Frontenac, the French made further punitive expeditions against the Iroquois and against the Dutch-English village of Schenectady as part of King William's War, the American theater of the 1689–1697 War of the Grand Alliance between France and an alliance of Emperor Leopold I, the Netherlands, and the English. By its close the situation had reached a stalemate. In the summer of 1701 the Five Nations made peace with the French at Montreal and were invited to trade with them at Detroit, and in return the Iroquois promised to remain neutral in case of further Franco-English wars. However, the Iroquois simultaneously renewed their Chain of Friendship with the English at Albany and by doing so entered a new policy of armed neutrality between the two colonial powers.

During much of the first half of the 18th century this neutrality held, despite the Delaware and Shawnee support of French interests at various times. During Queen Anne's War 1702–1713 (the American theater of the War of the Spanish Succession) and King George's War 1744–1748 (the American theater of the War of the Austrian Succession) the Iroquois helped the English colonies keep their frontier intact in spite of French and Indian raids from Canada in the north. They also extended their "Tree of Peace" to various refugee and remnant Indian groups at Conestoga, Paxtang, Shamokin, Wyoming, Wyalusing, Sheshequin, Tioga, and the Great Bend in the Susquehanna Valley, by so doing protecting the "Southern Door of the Longhouse." With the French missionaries now gone from Iroquoia, pastors of the Dutch Reformed Church and clergy of the Anglican faith made converts—particularly among the Mohawks, who remained in their traditional homes along the Mohawk River, devising a system of writing in the Mohawk language and providing schooling for children. In 1710 three Iroquois sachems (chiefs) and a Mohican visited London, were presented at court, and painted by Jan Verelst (see pages 26, 47, 137, and 139). They were also presented with sets of silver communion service plates for their church at Fort Hunter. Today, these are still used at churches in two communities in Ontario, Six Nations and Tyendinagaby—descendants of the New York Mohawks, who were forced to leave their village after the American Revolution.

Between 1713 and 1722 an Iroquoian-speaking tribe of North Carolina, the Tuscarora, requested to live among the Five Nations. The Tuscarora were admitted to the League as a Sixth Nation, so the Five Nations became the Six Nations about 1722. The Tuscarora now became near equals with the other tribes of the League. However, a number of smaller groups were adopted into the Confederacy as "Props to the Confederacy" and were controlled by the Iroquois through appointed emissaries—called Half Kings—throughout the Susquehanna Valley. These groups ultimately moved north to be fully absorbed into the Confederacy.

In 1738 a young Anglo-Irishman, William Johnson, arrived in the Mohawk Valley. He was subsequently to build a huge commercial empire from the fur trade and land speculation. He became firm friends of the local Mohawks whose villages were dotted among the white settlements: at Schenectady, established by the Dutch; Fort Hunter, an English fort and mission; German Flats settled by Palatines (Protestant refugees from the Rhineland, who had fled to England in the face of French attacks and of whom some 3,000 were shipped to New York in 1710); and Canajoharie, an Indian village with intermarried Europeans. Within a few years Johnson had built a fortress-like home, Mount Johnson, and had married into the Mohawks; his second wife was a niece of

"King Hendrick," once believed to have been one of the four sachems who had visited England in 1710. After her death he married Molly Brant, half-sister of Joseph Brant, step-grandchild of another of the leaders who had traveled to London in 1710, and destined to become a British war captain during the American Revolution.

In 1745 Johnson was appointed British Commissioner of Indian Affairs and in 1755 Superintendent of Indian Affairs by General Edward Braddock, the newly arrived British military commander, at the start of the French and Indian War (1754–1760)— that became part of the Seven Years War (1756–1763). Johnson's influence over the Mohawks was to have an important part to play in the forthcoming conflict. He had already established himself as an important trader and learned many aspects of Iroquois culture and ceremony by the time of the King George's War (1744–1748). He was organizing Mohawk war parties to attack the French and their Indian settlements in Canada and was involved in the grisly business of paying for enemy scalps—both Indian and European. The scalplock taken from an enemy's head was proof of valor and a token of spiritual power.

## THE FRENCH AND INDIAN WAR 1754–1760

In 1747 the Virginians organized the Ohio Company to look at expanding into the Ohio country bounded by the Great Kanawha and Ohio rivers and the Allegheny mountains, to colonize and trade with Indians and to sell land. Although some of the tribes of the area had been relocated from farther east—such as the Delawares and Mahicans—and were still connected to the Covenant Chain, the Shawnees were not. Pennsylvania, also interested in the area, made a treaty with some Miami Indians attracted to George Croghan's trading stronghold of Pickawillany. With the Iroquois influence on the Ohio Indians now waning, their half kings' duplicity, and the bribery of Pennsylvania's agents Croghan and Andrew Montour at Logstown to allow in traders and settlers, sparked the beginning of a general campaign by the French to sweep away all the Pennsylvania traders out of the region. In 1753 New France began building a chain of forts down the west side of the Alleghenies, moving from one strategic waterway to another with the objective of bringing the whole Ohio Valley under their control, climaxing with the building of Fort Duquesne at the Forks of the Ohio. A young Colonel George Washington was sent by the Ohio Company to make a treaty with the French but failed, and when a second military attempt also failed with surrender at Fort Necessity on July 4, 1754, the echoes were heard in Albany and even in London.

The Iroquois were not strong enough to stand alone in the west against the French and their growing numbers of Indian allies. The Grand Council at Onondaga had completely lost control of the Ohio Indians, and the Delawares in the west gloried in their independence from the Iroquois. The British response to the events in the Ohio Country was to send an army of 2,000 men under the command of General Edward Braddock of the Coldstream Guards, which hacked its way slowly through the forests to the banks of the Monongahela River (that merges with the Allegheny at the Forks of the Ohio) a few miles from Fort Duquesne where the column arrived on July 9, 1755. The French and Indians encircled Braddock's column firing from the thick cover of the woods. The British troops began a mass retreat and panic prevailed: over a thousand soldiers were killed in 2 hours with Braddock dying of his wounds later. The French had reminded the Delawares of old grievances; the loss in succession of their homelands in eastern Pennsylvania and then the beautiful Wyoming Valley, and as a result the Delawares sent out war parties from both their eastern and western branches. To restore Pennsylvania's morale a raid led by Colonel John Armstrong against

**Above:** Sir William Johnson (1715–1774). Johnson commanded Iroquois and colonial militia forces during the French and Indian War, the North American theater of the Seven Years War, first as a colonel then as a Major General for the British during the French and Indian War. After the Indian Department was established in 1755 to oversee relations between the government of the United Kingdom of Great Britain and Ireland and those First Nations in British North America, he became the Superintendent of Indian Affairs, a position he held until his death.

**Opposite:** John of Canajoharie, a Mohawk chief and one of the Four Kings at the court of Queen Anne in 1710. Note the belt, perhaps moosehair embroidery, probably the same as worn by the other kings in the three other paintings by Verelst in the National Archives of Canada.

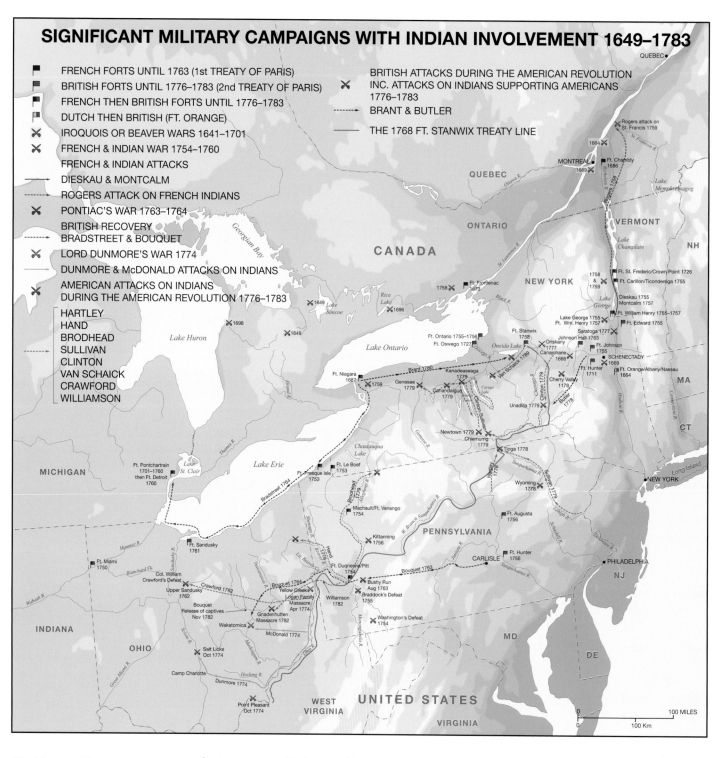

# SIGNIFICANT MILITARY CAMPAIGNS WITH INDIAN INVOLVEMENT 1649–1783

⚑ FRENCH FORTS UNTIL 1763 (1st TREATY OF PARIS)

⚑ BRITISH FORTS UNTIL 1776–1783 (2nd TREATY OF PARIS)

⚑ FRENCH THEN BRITISH FORTS UNTIL 1776–1783

⚑ DUTCH THEN BRITISH (FT. ORANGE)

✕ IROQUOIS OR BEAVER WARS 1641–1701

✕ FRENCH & INDIAN WAR 1754–1760

FRENCH & INDIAN ATTACKS

— DIESKAU & MONTCALM

- - - ROGERS ATTACK ON FRENCH INDIANS

✕ PONTIAC'S WAR 1763–1764

BRITISH RECOVERY
- - - BRADSTREET & BOUQUET

✕ LORD DUNMORE'S WAR 1774

— DUNMORE & McDONALD ATTACKS ON INDIANS

✕ AMERICAN ATTACKS ON INDIANS
DURING THE AMERICAN REVOLUTION 1776–1783

HARTLEY
HAND
BRODHEAD
SULLIVAN
CLINTON
VAN SCHAICK
CRAWFORD
WILLIAMSON

✕ BRITISH ATTACKS DURING THE AMERICAN REVOLUTION
INC. ATTACKS ON INDIANS SUPPORTING AMERICANS
1776–1783

- - - BRANT & BUTLER

— THE 1768 FT. STANWIX TREATY LINE

Significant military campaigns with Indian involvement, 1649–1783.

the western Delawares' base at Kittanning caused them to withdraw their settlements to Beaver Creek. The Iroquois were still unwilling or unable to control the Delawares on the western flank of Iroquoia until at the Easton Treaty of October 1758, climaxing a long campaign of diplomatic pressure, the Six Nations finally brought Teedyuscung, the Delaware leader, to heel.

Although the Confederacy as a whole remained neutral during the conflict, there was little doubt some Senecas were acting with the Delaware and Shawnees in the west. However, in the east Sir William Johnson's expert management of British relationships with the Mohawks had once more raised them to pre-eminence in the Iroquois League. He revived the Covenant Chain and in time-honored custom of Indian traders marrying into prestigious chiefly families, he had children with first Elizabeth Brant and, in the 1760s, Molly Brant. He had been given instructions by Braddock to manage the affairs of the Six Nations and his function as Indian Superintendent was to recruit Indian auxiliaries to fight against the French. Braddock's defeat had left the British plans in a shambles; at least the Mohawks, allowed to act alone, were favorably disposed to side with them in the conflict along the upper Hudson River Valley which was already in French hands and long claimed to be their territory.

In 1755 William Johnson with 2,000 men began a march north along the Hudson River in a bold campaign directed at driving the French from Fort St. Frederic on Lake Champlain. The building of Fort Lyman (later named Fort Edward) was begun and Johnson moved on to the head of Lake St. Sacrement, which he renamed Lake George in honor of George II, by the end of August 1755. In the meantime a French expedition under the German Baron de Dieskau had set out south from Fort St. Frederic (later Crown Point) to Fort Carillon (later Ticonderoga). From there he promptly embarked in canoes on Lake Champlain with 216 French regulars, 684 Canadians, and 600 Indians. Landing at South Bay (Whitehall), Dieskau force-marched overland with a plan to attack Fort Lyman. However, the plan was changed and instead he began to assault Johnson's position on Lake George. Johnson's Indian scouts had brought him news of Dieskau's movements and he dispatched 1,000 men under Colonel Ephraim Williams, along with King Hendrick and his Mohawks, to intercept the French, but they were ambushed at Rocky Brook a mere 3 miles from Johnson's camp. Both Williams and Hendrick were killed. The survivors of the ambush reached Johnson's camp closely pursued by the French. The assault on the entrenched provincials' position was halted with heavy losses and the wounded Dieskau was taken prisoner. A force of 250 men commanded by Colonel Blanchard from Fort Lyman came upon several hundred Canadians and Indians near Rocky Brook. Attacking fiercely, the colonials killed many and bodies were thrown into the water, which has ever since been known as Bloody Pond. So ended the battle of Lake George: effectively three separate engagements with both sides losing over 300 men. It was a victory for the English colonies in a year marked by defeats elsewhere. However, Johnson abandoned his campaign against Fort St. Frederic but remained at the head of Lake George where he built Fort William Henry, named after one of the grandsons of King George II.

William Johnson saves Baron de Dieskau during the Battle of Lake George in 1755. From a painting attributed to Benjamin West, Derby Museum, UK.

In March 1757 the French from Fort Carillon (Ticonderoga), with Canadian and Indian militia, attacked Fort William Henry over the frozen surface of the lake in a surprise attack. The garrison of 346 British troops and rangers survived the assault. The area around Lake George became the scene of many skirmishes between the French and their Indian allies and the colonial American forest rangers operating from Forts William Henry and Edward. Notable among the rangers were Robert Rogers and Israel Putnam conducting forays against the French in the vicinity of Fort St. Frederic and Fort Carillon. A notable engagement was the so-called Battle on Snowshoes on March 13, 1758, when Rogers and his rangers were found and attacked by a much greater number of French and Indians. The remnants of Rogers' force reached Fort Edward after a running fight that saw 125 rangers killed.

However, the fate of Fort William Henry had already been sealed the previous August when the French with a force of 6,000 regulars and Canadians and 1,700 Indians appeared before the fort having come down from Fort Carillon. The French, under their commander the Marquis de Montcalm, bombarded the fort until the British commander, Colonel George Monro, agreed to surrender despairing of any help from Fort Edward.

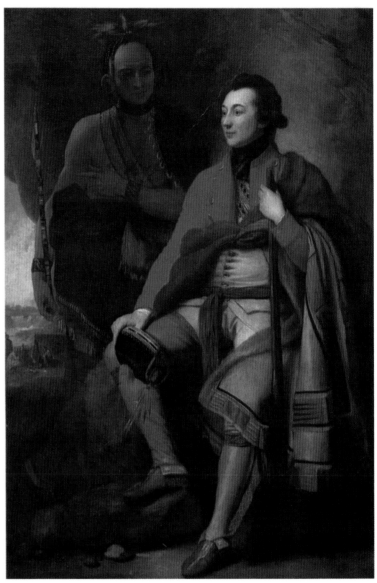

**Above:** The statue of King Hendrick and Sir William Johnson erected in the State Park, Lake George, NY, to commemorate the victory over the French in September 1755. Hendrick was killed and Johnson wounded in the battle.

On the morning of August 10, 1757, the surrendered British forces marched out on the road to Fort Edward but the column was attacked by the Indians who killed 50 men, women, and children and carried off 200 as prisoners—they were later taken back to Canada. Except for the intervention of Montcalm himself, many more would have been killed. Montcalm had Fort William Henry burned to the ground and he returned to Fort Carillon on August 16.

In July 1758 an army of 15,000 British regulars and colonials under General James Abercromby embarked in a huge flotilla and moved north for an assault on Fort Carillon. In the battle that followed, Montcalm again defeated the British and inflicted heavy losses. The following year another expedition under Sir Jeffrey Amherst finally seized Fort Carillon and Fort St. Frederic from the French. Fort Carillon was now renamed Ticonderoga and Fort St. Frederic, Crown Point by Amherst. The British capture of Louisbourg at the second attempt had given them control of the St. Lawrence River. Meanwhile Fort Frontenac fell to Colonel Bradstreet in August 1758, and in the west an expedition led by Brigadier-General John Forbes with a nearly 5,000-strong army of Scottish Highlanders, Germans, and Cherokee warriors marched to the Forks of

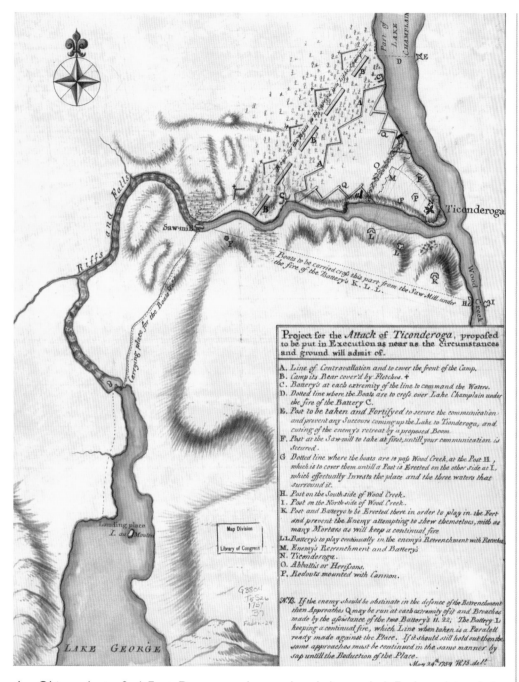

**Far left:** Colonel Guy Johnson, nephew and son-in-law of Sir William Johnson. The background Indian figure is likely to be Capt. David Hill (Karonghyontye), or his brother Lt. John Hill, all members of a party who went to London in 1775. The party also included Daniel Claus, John Dease, Joseph Brant, and others including Ethan Allen, an American prisoner. Painting by Benjamin West in England.

**Left:** "Project for the attack of Ticonderoga, proposed to be put in execution as near as the circumstances and ground will admit of." Prepared by William Brasier, a draftsman in the British Army. The map, dated May 29, 1759, says (capitals and misspellings as the original): "If the enemy should be obstinate in the defence of the Retrenchment then Approaches Q may be run at each extremity of it, and breaches made by the assistance of the two Battery's 11. 22. The Battery L keeping a continual fire, which Line when taken is a Paralell ready made against the Place. If it should still hold out then the same approaches must be continued in the same manner by sap untill the Reduction of the Place."

the Ohio only to find Fort Duquesne deserted and dismantled. Forbes claimed the ruins and renamed it Fort Pitt after the British Prime Minister William Pitt. Sir William Johnson, despite being wounded at Lake George, led regulars, provincials, and 900 Iroquois warriors to victory at Fort Niagara in July 1759, and General Wolfe won his decisive battle at Quebec in September of the same year. Amherst finally captured Montreal in September 1760 effectively ending the conflict between Britain and France in North America, although fighting continued elsewhere.

The defeat of the French in North America was ratified by the 1763 Treaty of Paris by which France forfeited everything east of the Mississippi except for the enclave around New Orleans. The Mohawks had played a major supporting role in the British victory. Wolfe, Bradstreet, Johnson, and Rogers were the heroes, but Washington, who had opened hostilities, was for now a forgotten man.

**Above:** Sychnecta. A drawing of a Mohawk visitor to Europe in 1764. Note the pipe-tomahawk, gorgets and snowshoes. From a drawing and etching apparently done in Amsterdam.

**Above right:** Johnson Hall, Johnstown, NY, completed in 1763 and home of William Johnson and his Mohawk third wife, Molly Brant, until his death in 1774. It was here Johnson held many meetings with the sachems of the Iroquois and other tribes. The hall is now restored as a museum. Photographed in 1987.

## NEW WARS IN THE NORTHWEST

In the spring of 1763 a new war broke out in the west. The British, now in control of the western forts, abandoned the French practice of distributing presents to the Indians, including food in winter and powder and shot for hunting. This was on the orders of General Amherst, the British Commander-in-Chief who was tightening American expenditure at London's demand following the expensive war recently concluded. Also Amherst had a dislike and distrust of Indians and his actions seemed deliberately to provoke them. Efforts of sturdy frontiersmen such as Croghan, Claus, Montour, and McKee failed to appease the western tribes, who had enjoyed the camaraderie of the French trappers and mixed bloods and who were still wandering freely. Hostilities were organized by the Ottawa Chief Pontiac, who led a remarkable coalition of tribes, including Ottawas, Ojibwas, Potawatomis, Shawnees, Mingos, and Wyandots (reformed Hurons in the Ohio Country).

The situation was not promising. After the long wars the Indians faced grave economic problems. Crops had not been managed, women demanded French finery, and they had little ammunition. Amherst actually urged Colonel Henry Bouquet to spread smallpox among the tribes about to attack. The coalition attacked and captured Forts Sandusky, Miami, Ouiatenon, and after a famous game of lacrosse, they stormed Michilimackinac. Later, when joined by some Senecas, they captured Forts Venango, Le Boeuf, and Presque Isle (Erie). In all, eight forts were captured of the 12 in Indian country; another was abandoned and Forts Pitt and Detroit were under siege. However, Pontiac was unable to keep his warriors together, and the British retaliated with Colonel Bradstreet reinforcing Detroit and Colonel Bouquet outmaneuvring the hostiles during an ambush at Bushy Run en route to relieve Fort Pitt in August 1763. The winter of 1763–1764 was particularly harsh on the Indians and with the approval of the new commander-in-chief, General Thomas Gage, Sir William Johnson used his Mohawk agents to bring the renegade Seneca sachems to Johnson Hall to agree to peace; splits were already

appearing in the Indian coalition. In need of food and supplies more Indians parleyed with Johnson at Niagara with inconclusive results. In August 1764 Colonel Bradstreet gave peace terms to the natives, and in October, Bouquet took a strong force west to the Tuscarawas River and then, by November, to the Forks of the Muskingum River, forcing the Delawares, Shawnees, Mingos, and Caughnawagas to give up their white prisoners. The war gradually came to an end when Pontiac's followers were overawed by this display of British force and the chief concluded a peace treaty in 1766 at Oswego, NY with William Johnson.

In 1768 the Six Nations and the Seven Nations of Canada met in a general congress at Johnson Hall, and later George Croghan met Delawares, Shawnees, and Wyandots at Fort Pitt. The conclusion was a major treaty signed at Fort Stanwix (Rome, NY) held by Sir William Johnson and the aforementioned tribes, together with the governor of New Jersey, commissioners from Virginia and Pennsylvania, and officials of other colonies. A firm boundary was agreed between the colonies and the Indian nations, negotiated and a deed of cession made. The old Covenant Chain was renewed and strengthened and large presents were given to the Indians. However, the general peace was fragile and Johnson feared another western confederacy having clandestine French instigation and support. He assembled several meetings to confer with chiefs of many tribes about the continuing troubles in the Ohio Country, and at one such meeting in 1774 he died. Pontiac himself was murdered in Cahokia, Illinois in 1769.

In 1774 Lord Dunmore of Virginia, ignoring the Royal Proclamation of 1763, issued land warrants to the veterans of the French and Indian War to allow them to settle west of the Allegheny mountains, and a gang of Virginians massacred Logan's Mingos, friends of the Shawnees, and occupied the abandoned Fort Pitt. The Iroquois protested vigorously to William Johnson, who died in the midst of the controversy. Chief Cornstalk surprised the Virginians at Point Pleasant at the junction of the Ohio and the Great Kanawahe rivers, but was beaten off, and Cornstalk later made peace with Dunmore, accepting the Ohio River as the new boundary of Shawnee lands.

**Above:** A plaque to the "intrepid warrior" Pontiac, organizer of the conspiracy which bears his name in May 1763.

**Above left:** A plaque to the Shawnee chief, Cornstalk, "celebrated for his leadership of an Indian army against Virginia volunteers under Colonel Andrew Lewis, in the Battle of Point Pleasant, Virginia, October 10, 1774. Although they destroyed one-fifth of Lewis's forces, the Indians retreated and made peace with Lord Dunmore, Governor of Virginia, at Camp Charlotte, a few miles east of Cornstalk's town."

**Above:** Silver presentation type pipe-tomahawk made for the Duke of Northumberland and due to be given to Joseph Brant on the occasion of his third visit to London in 1805. However he did not arrive due to lack of funds.

**Right:** Joseph Brant by Gilbert Stuart, 1786. Brant had visited London to petition the British authorities for protection of land rights in Upper Canada. He wears a striking costume that combines native regalia with English silver adornment, including an ornamental collar awarded by the king.

## THE AMERICAN REVOLUTION AND THE AFTERMATH

The first shots fired at Lexington on April 19, 1775, would give birth to the United States and would bring to an end the Iroquois Confederacy as a significant political and military power. The British Parliament set up the Quebec Act for the conquered province of Canada and established Quebec's government control over the "crown lands" of Indian country north of the Ohio River, thus destroying all hope of expansion into these territories by Virginia, Massachusetts, and Connecticut. This with the well-known taxation and representation problems led to revolution. Though the chiefs tried to maintain neutrality, agents of the crown and colonists worked on the sachems of the separate tribes so that consensus became impossible. The League was suspended and individual tribal councils made independent decisions either to remain neutral or decide to fight for one side, the Tories, loyal to the British Crown, or the other, the American revolutionaries. The Mohawks, Onondagas, Cayugas, and Senecas mostly joined the British, while the Oneidas and Tuscaroras joined the Americans. With the end of the League's supervision over their tributary Indians, the western Delawares also decided for the Americans.

The Mohawks, in particular, under John Johnson (William's son by Catherine Weisenberg), Guy Johnson (William's nephew), and the Mohawk Joseph Brant with the support of Colonel John Butler and his son, Lt. Walter Butler, were active in raids on the American frontier settlements. In November 1775 Brant accompanied Guy Johnson to London, the first of two visits, where King George III conferred upon him the rank of captain. On his return he became the scourge of the American settlements in New York and Pennsylvania where he was associated with atrocities which occurred at Wyoming, PA, Kingston, PA, and Cherry Valley, Otsego County, NY in 1778—although he was probably not even present at Wyoming. However, their incursions and other raids in the Cherry and Mohawk valleys were devastating and part of a cycle of atrocity and counter-atrocity in which the Johnsons, Brant, and Butlers had gained an odious reputation among the revolutionary Patriots.

By 1777 the League had suspended its "fire," which had burned at Onondage since the founding of the Confederacy at least 250 years before, and moved it to Buffalo Creek. After the war it went to the Six Nations Reserve on the Grand River in Canada. In 1779 General Washington ordered the invasion of Iroquoia by two armies, one under Brigadier-General James Clinton, the other under Major-General John Sullivan. They destroyed all the hostile villages along the Genesee River and huge amounts of food, forcing the Senecas back to Fort Niagara. Although Brant continued to raid American settlements and burned Oneida and Tuscarora villages in retaliation for their support of the Americans, the tide of war turned against the British. In 1779, Brant visited Quebec and London and obtained assurances from Governor Haldimand that lands in Canada would be found for Iroquois who had remained loyal to the Crown. In September 1783 at the Treaty of Paris, Great Britain ceded sovereignty to the United States over all territory east of the Mississippi, although the Iroquois were omitted from consideration.

During 1784–1785, Brant's Mohawks, who had moved from Canajoharie to Niagara and had conducted their raids from that location, moved to the Grand River where they were joined by a large number of Cayugas and a few representatives of the other Iroquois nations. Brant lived the remainder of his life at Burlington, Ontario close to the city which now bears his name—Brantford. A second group of Mohawks, originally from Fort Hunter, NY, who had operated from Lachine near Montreal under John Deseronto and Aaron and Isaac Hill also found a home in Canada on the shores of the Bay of Quinte—now the reserve of Tyendinaga. Those Iroquois who now remained on American soil were forced under duress into treaties the United States imposed by right of conquest at Forts Stanwix (1784), Herkimer (1785), Harmar (1789), Canandaigua (1794), and after the defeat of the western tribes, Greenville (1795).

## DISINTEGRATION, REFORMATION, AND PERSEVERANCE: 1783 TO THE PRESENT

At the Treaty of Paris signed by the new United States and Great Britain in 1783, no provisions were made for the Iroquois who had fought for the crown. However Haldimand, Brant, and Simcoe pressured the British government to approve their earlier assurances that compensatory lands would be provided in Canada. Consequently, the Six Nations Reserve was created along the Grand River and the Tyendinaga Reserve on the Bay of Quinte. Those who remained within the borders of the new United

Sa-go-ye-wat-ha—the Seneca chief Red Jacket—painted by R.W. Weir and engraved by M. J. Danforth between 1830 and 1880. On his chest he wears the silver medal presented by George Washington (see also page 142).

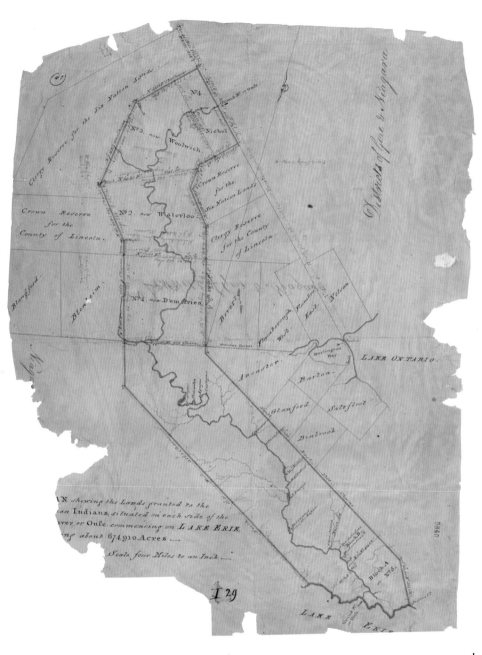

States were left at the mercy of the new American administration. The Iroquois were forced to agree to the second treaty of Fort Stanwix in 1784 and another at Canandaigua in 1794, which no longer recognized the old 1768 Stanwix Treaty and the boundary line between the British colonies and the Ohio Valley tribes. Settlers and land speculators who flooded into the old northwest sought to extinguish the land rights beyond the Ohio River. The Iroquois were not strong enough to join in the new war which broke out as a consequence involving the Miamis, Shawnees, and Wyandots, which ended with their defeat and agreement to the Treaty of Greenville of 1795. Chief Cornplanter, who had been responsible for keeping the Iroquois out of this conflict, encouraged friendship with the Americans and some of his followers adopted the white man's lifestyle at his model community in northern Pennsylvania. In 1798 he brought in Quaker teachers and established schools, although he became disillusioned with white men in later life and destroyed gifts he had received from them. He died in 1836.

The very rapidly shrinking reservation populations witnessed a consequent loss of morale, with idleness, drunkenness, violence, and family instability. Former warriors were forced to take up farming, normally the preserve of their women, and hunting was restricted by the reduced size of reservation lands. In 1799 Cornplanter's half-brother, Handsome Lake (Ganiodariyo or Skanyadario), had a vision from the Creator (through the Three Messengers) with instructions on how to revitalize the Iroquois with moral and social reform, with a strong stance against alcohol abuse and witchcraft. His teachings merged Iroquois traditional cosmology with new elements, a heaven and hell, but also endorsing traditional practices such as the Midwinter Ceremony and obligations to kinship. He clearly had been influenced by the Quakers, and their Protestant-type ethic of personal responsibility. His followers launched a religious movement which spread throughout the Iroquois world, preaching a strict morality and restoring a pride in their race. The "Good Word (or Message)," which he received in his visions, became the basis of the New Religion and their "Keepers of the Faith" still even today conduct periodical meetings of several days of public worship, of prayers, thanksgiving, confession, religious dancing, and the recitation of the "Code of Handsome Lake." The story of his career and a collection of his sermons and sayings, are today recited by professional orators.

Map showing the Haldimand Tract along the Grand River in Upper Canada, granted to the Six Nations Confederacy in 1784. This version is a survey of the Six Nations Indian lands completed in 1821.

Three Huron chiefs residing at the village-reserve at La Jeune Lorette, near Quebec, by Edward Chatfield, 1825. They wear European style coats, woven sashes, moccasins, metal earrings, armbands, bracelets, and medals. During the 18th century the Hurons of Lorette joined two Abenaki groups and the Iroquois of Caughnawaga, Oka, St. Regis, and Oswegatchie as "The Seven Nations of Canada" and allies of the French.

This religion, containing elements of both traditional and Christian values codified as the Longhouse Religion, has become, and still remains, a force for the maintenance of Iroquois identity and unity. Many present-day Iroquois find nothing inconsistent in attendance at both Church and Longhouse services.

During the early 19th century private land companies took advantage of Indian factionalism and successfully whittled away the Iroquois domain in western New York. The lands of the Oneidas were reduced to such a few acres that many moved to lands purchased from the Menomini Indians of Wisconsin under the direction of their Mohawk minister Eleazar Williams, or to the Thames River, Ontario (Oneidatown). The Cayugas sold almost all their lands around Cayuga Lake and went to live with the Senecas and Onondaga. In the 1830s the US government had a policy of forcing all Indian people east of the Mississippi to move to Indian Territory (now Oklahoma) and a small number of Seneca of Sandusky and Cayuga from Ohio and New York, combined as the Seneca-Cayuga and moved to live in Oklahoma. In 1838 the Ogden Land Company used dubious means to negotiate a teaty depriving the Senecas of all their lands in western New York. However, Rev. Asher Wright, a missionary among the Senecas, and the Society of Friends produced evidence of fraud, bribery, and forgery, and by 1842 had regained the Allegany and Cattaraugus reservations; additionally, in 1858 the Senecas repurchased the Tonawanda Reservation. These reservations, together with Onondaga, Tuscarora, and St. Regis, formed the New York reservations

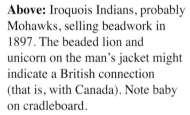

**Above:** Iroquois Indians, probably Mohawks, selling beadwork in 1897. The beaded lion and unicorn on the man's jacket might indicate a British connection (that is, with Canada). Note baby on cradleboard.

**Above center:** Iroquois family on tour in England, c. 1870. The man wears an Iroquois-style bandolier pouch.

**Above right:** Iroquois family probably from Caughnawaga wearing beaded collars with designs of birds, flags, and stars c. 1880.

and have survived to the present day. The Oneida lands, hitherto reduced to a few acres, have recently been increased by purchases funded by their successful casino operation. However, federal and state pressure resulted in the loss of the Cornplanter grant in Pennsylvania for the Kinzna Dam project, and legal battles in defence of lands on the Tuscarora Reservation. In Canada the Oka Indians fought to save a graveyard threatened by a golf club expansion in 1990–1991.

The descendants of the Iroquois won over to French interest in the 17th century settled at the old Catholic missions at St. Regis, Caughnawaga, and Oka were gradually re-establishing contact with their New York and Six Nations relatives who had once expelled them from the League. They had sided with the French during the long period of colonial warfare, and refused to side with the British during the American Revolution, although urged to do so by Joseph Brant and Sir Guy Carleton. Some joined the Colonial army—such as Louis Cook, a St. Regis Mohawk who rose to the rank of captain. During the War of 1812, the last time the Iroquois took up the hatchet, Iroquois from Six Nations Reserve fought with the British at Niagara, Buffalo, and Brantford under John Brant, and St. Regis was disturbed by incursions from both American and British troops. In the late 18th and early 19th centuries a number of Iroquois men from Caughnawaga, St. Regis, and Oka joined the Hudson's Bay and North West fur companies as trappers in the far west. Others were noted for being especially brave and skilled craftsmen and river pilots and some were hired by the British government for the Gordon relief expedition in the Sudan in 1884.

In 1886 when a bridge was being erected across the St. Lawrence River men from Caughnawaga (Kahnawake) were hired to help in the construction work. So adept did these workers become as steelwork erectors they, and generations ever since, have become renowned in that industry with many skyscrapers erected by gangs of specialist fixers.

By the 1850s schooling had begun to benefit new generations of Iroquois people who were developing skills in business, attending colleges, and becoming self-sufficient farmers. Although farming has been replaced by an off-reservation wage economy, perhaps 50,000 people of Iroquois descent still live on, or near, their reserves in Canada and the United States, with as many again in the great cities. They are still Haudenosaunee— People of the Longhouse—although few, if any, are of full Iroquois descent, which is not surprising after nearly five centuries of European contact, adoption, and intermarriage with both whites and other Indian tribes. Today, perhaps 2,000 Mohawk have retained their language on the Canadian reserves. However, scarcely more than a few dozen elderly people in each of the other five tribes are fluent in their native tongues. Casinos have also brought wealth to a number of Iroquois communities. In 1988 employment on the small 13-acre Oneida Reservation in New York with its bingo hall and smoke shop was just seven people. Today, their Turning Stone Casino alone offers work for 3,000 employees.

## IROQUOIS IN THE WEST

In the late 18th century the North West Fur Company, competitors of the Hudson's Bay Company, employed a number of eastern Indians, including Iroquois men, as trappers and boatmen in the foothills of the Rockies in present-day Alberta. These Indians proved to be successful trappers of beavers using steel traps, whereas the local Indians were still using more primitive devices. Most of these Iroquois men were Mohawks from Caughnawaga and St. Regis, who married Cree and Metis women, and were hunting and living around the Grande Cache area. Later they moved to the Catholic mission at Lac St. Anne and in 1880 moved to the Michel's Reserve at Callihoo near Riviere Qui Barre but had lost their Iroquois traditions and language. In 1958 they renounced their legal status as Indians, the reserve was abolished and they are no longer registered as

**Below left:** Indian Territory, now Oklahoma, with (below right) detail showing the location of the area settled by the Seneca-Cayuga in 1831, after they had sold their lands in Ohio.

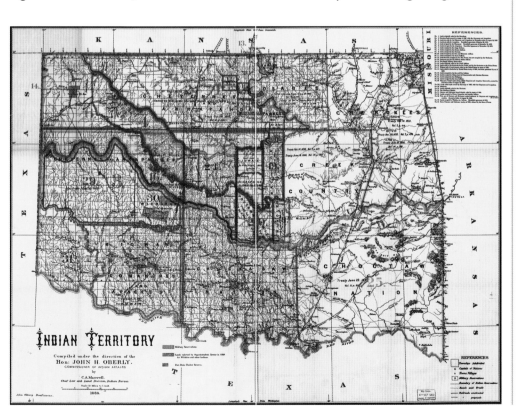

Canadian natives. Other Iroquois pioneers in the American far west have been reported from Oregon and intermarried with a number of Plateau tribes. Several Iroquois men were hired by the trader David Thompson in 1810 and their descendants settled on the Salish-Kutenai (Flathead) Reservation in western Montana. The artist Gustavus Sohon sketched several Iroquois men amongst the Flatheads in 1854 and Alfred Jacob Miller painted a buckskin-clad Iroquois man probably at the Green River Rendezvous, present day Wyoming, in 1837.

**Left:** Charles Lamoose, son of Ignace Lamoose, leader of the Iroquois living with the Flatheads of Montana. Charles was half Iroquois and half Pend d'Oreille, and typical of dozens of Iroquois who were intermarried with western tribes during the 19th century. Drawn by Gustavus Sohon in 1854.

**Below:** Iroquois men, Six Nations Reserve, Ontario c. 1890. Note many men are wearing braided and beaded sashes, feather headdresses, and a number also wear native-style cloth leggings.

**Right:** Six Nations survivors of the War of 1812—an 1882 studio portrait taken in Brantford of (left to right): Sakawaraton John "Smoke" Johnson, John Tutelo, and Young Warner.

# Chapter 2: Culture

**Opposite:** Interior and exterior views of an Iroquois bark home.

**Below:** John Danford, Canadian Oneida chief, wears a cloth coat with collar, front opening, and cuffs decorated with fine beadwork. He also has a beaded shoulder bag, leggings, and moccasins. He holds a bow and arrows and a steel pipe-tomahawk. Photographed by an unknown photographer, c. 1900.

## IROQUOIS SOCIAL AND POLITICAL ORGANIZATION

A typical Iroquois village was a cluster of 30–50 dome or peaked-shaped bark longhouses surrounded by a palisade usually on a raised area of land accessible to drinking water and near a small river or lake. Each family or "fireside" of husband, wife, and children belonged to a residential group related through the female line (matrilineal clans). Each clan had a head woman, mother, or matron who was responsible for the appointments of the Confederacy Chiefs in accordance with the instructions given by the founders of the League at its conception. Each clan was identified with an animal, bird, or reptile that served as its crest which was displayed on the gable ends of a longhouse or tattooed on the chests of its members. Marriage was forbidden between members of the same clan, so when a man took a wife the children became members of their mother's clan. The clans of each tribe were divided into two halves or "moieties," each of which carried out distinctive ritualistic and social functions.

The League itself was also divided into moieties: the Mohawk, Onondaga, and Seneca were the "older brothers" and the Oneida, Cayuga, and Tuscarora, the "younger brothers." Although some variations have been reported, the arrangement of the clans and moieties were as follows:

*Older brothers*
Mohawk had three clans:
Moiety A — Wolf and Bear
Moiety B — Turtle

Onondaga had nine clans:
Moiety A — Wolf, Tortoise (Turtle), Snipe, Eagle, and Beaver
Moiety B — Deer, Bear, Hawk, and Eel

Seneca had nine clans:
Moiety A — Turtle, Wolf, Bear, Beaver, and Heron
Moiety B — Snipe, Deer, Hawk, and Eel

*Younger brothers*
Oneida had three clans:
Moiety A — Wolf
Moiety B — Turtle and Bear

Cayuga had 10 clans:
Moiety A — Heron, Wolf, Plover, Hawk, and Snipe
Moiety B — Deer, Ball, Turtle, and two Bear clans

Tuscarora had seven clans:
Moiety A — Wolf and Bear
Moiety B — Turtle, Beaver, Deer, Eel, and Snipe

Iroquois man wearing buckskin coat, leggings, headdress, and a bandolier bag of a Delaware type, c. 1850–1860. Photograph c. 1880.

Moiety A was sometimes called the Wolf Moiety and B the Turtle or Deer Moiety from their leading clans. The centrally located Onondaga were usually responsible for calling the Grand or Federal Councils of the five tribes, who had agreed and confirmed the original concept of the "Great Peace" or "Great Law." However, among the Six Nations in Canada, the Tuscarora have been allowed to provide Confederacy Chiefs from their clans.

The Iroquois hereditary Confederacy Chiefs elected by the clan mothers from each tribe were called Rotiyaner (the Beloved Ones) or Peace Chiefs. These 50 hereditary sachems and their titles date from the conception of the League, with an additional 13 Tuscarora chiefs added later among the Grand River (Six Nations) Iroquois in Canada when the Confederacy reformed after the Revolution. The assistants to the Peace Chiefs with some executive powers were the Warrior or War chiefs or Ratikowanes, glossed the "Great Ones" and below them were Pine Tree Chiefs, men or women who shone above the ordinary folk in either war, diplomacy, or oratory, and allowed to sit in the League's national councils. Traditionally the 50 hereditary chiefs were made up of 9 Mohawk, 9 Oneida, 14 Onondaga, 8 Seneca, and 10 Cayuga. After the Tuscarora joined as a sixth nation after 1722, their affairs were the responsibility of the Oneidas — their sponsors. The unequal numbers of Peace Chiefs and Warrior Chiefs from the various tribes may be due to some clans becoming extinct in early times. These arrangements can be shown diagrammatically in plans of a Longhouse Council meeting which can be viewed as a microcosm of Iroquoia itself — see diagram below.

In ancient and colonial times, War and Pine Tree chiefs, who were not voting members of the Confederacy Council, often acted as ambassadors of "half kings" to various tributary tribes as well as messengers and war captains. Today after four and a half centuries this traditional form of government still survives in Ontario, Canada (Six Nations Reserve) and New York State, although effectively only in vestige and ceremonial form. In 1924 the Canadian government, through the agency at Six Nations, recognized only a conventionally elected form of council which would thenceforth be allowed executive power, thus forming a schism which continues

## THE LEAGUE COUNCIL

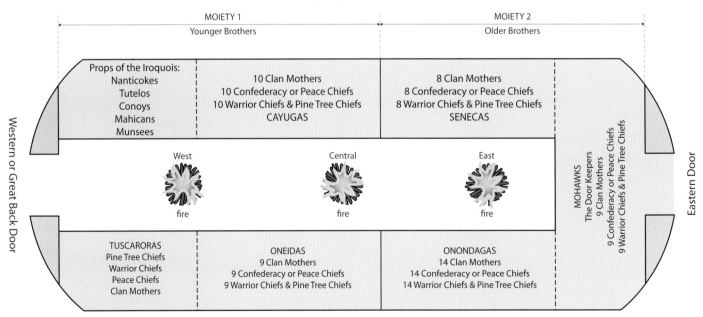

There were 50 hereditary titled Confederacy or Peace Chiefs, 1–50, as follows:
9 Mohawk Nos 1–9 (No 2 is Hiawatha or Ayonhwatha)
9 Oneida Nos 10–18
14 Onondaga nos 19–32 (No 19 is Thadodaho)
10 Cayuga Nos 33–42
8 Seneca Nos 43–50

The Ojibwa wife of the Canadian Oneida chief John Danford photographed at Muncey Town, Thames River, Ontario, in 1907. She wears a typical Iroquois cloth dress, cape, and pouch.

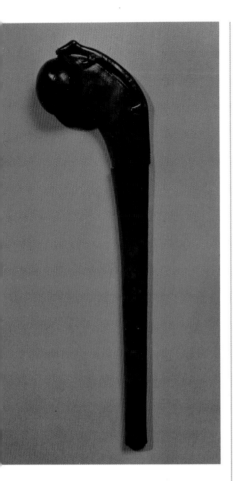

**Above:** Ball-headed club, eastern Great Lakes, early 19th century, possibly Iroquois. Narrower and lighter than many older examples, it may have been purely ceremonial. It has cut-out and carved designs and a human face on the ball head.

**Opposite:** Nicholas, a Mahican Indian (also called Mohican or River Indian), one of the "Four Kings" who came to London with the three Mohawks to seek support for an expedition against French Canada. Called Etow Oh Koam, he holds a ball-headed club, wears a quillwork belt and moccasins. His totemic symbol, a turtle, is shown on the ground. Painted by Jan Verelst in 1710 in London.

today and which sometimes results in non-cooperation with Canadian government officials.

Upon the death of a Confederacy sachem (one of the 50), his title was held in abeyance by the chief's clan-mother and a Great Council convened as a Condolence Council to mourn the deceased but also to appoint a successor. Today, as the League is split between New York and Canada, such councils may be held at Onondaga or Six Nations. The Condolence Council was a unique Iroquois ritual and ceremonial for the honor of deceased Confederacy Chiefs and for "raising up" their successors. In colonial times the ritual was also used for renewing colonial and tribal alliances, and for restoring fractured friendships and treaties, such as renewing the Covenant Chain with the British or making treaties of friendship with the French following periods of conflict. At such a meeting or conference the Iroquois chiefs present would act out a drama that would "strengthen the house." Such rituals of renewal would be acted out with colonial officials.

The pattern of the rituals divided those in despair or mourning from those who were clear-minded. An example in the English records concerns eight Mohawk sachems who came to Albany in 1690 to condole the survivors of the Schenectady massacre inflicted by the French and their Indian allies from Canada. After the Revolution the Americans refused to continue to participate in these rituals.

These Condolence ceremonies consisted of a program usually of 15 or 16 ritual parts, the important elements being the Roll Call, or Eulogy, of the 50 Confederacy Chiefs and titles serving to remind those present of the Laws of the Confederacy and its founders. Two other important rites of the ceremony are concerned with mourning: the Condoling Song, the great hymn of farewell to the deceased chief; and the Requickening Address, which is concerned with the symbolic power to restore well-being and "lift up" those depressed, to wipe away tears, to remove obstructions to various parts of the body and to dispel grief symbolically by the presentation of wampum strings to the bereaved moiety. The bereaved moiety (Oneida, Cayuga, and Tuscarora) was condoled by the clear-minded (Mohawk, Onondaga, and Seneca) or vice versa dependant upon to which moiety the dead chief belonged. Condolence rituals were also carried out for lesser chiefs (tribal chiefs) and lesser personalities with the ceremonial acted out by the two tribal moieties replacing those of the League.

## WARFARE

War Chiefs or Warrior Chiefs were separate from civil sachems. The selection depended upon great personal courage and military knowledge. While there could be no Confederacy warfare without the League's sanction, separate tribal action often took place particularly by the Mohawk and Seneca. War parties were recruited from among the young men, including the sons and grandsons of the Warrior Chiefs or former chiefs. Before taking to the warpath the participants were ritually purified, feasted, and danced about a war post symbolically striped with red paint. Women took no part in war ceremonies nor did the clans as such participate.

Ambush and surprise attacks were the feature of forest warfare. Scalps and prisoners were sought, the latter often being tortured and burned at the home village, but adoption of captives was common in order to replace relatives killed in war. Adoption was in the hands of women. Records of contemporary priests (the *Relations des jésuites*, the annual documents sent from the Canadian Jesuit mission to its Paris office, 1632–1672) tell us the Iroquois of the 17th century were particularly warlike and aggressive. An underlying economic motive seems to have driven them to expansion for monopoly in the fur trade and to hold the balance of power between European powers — Dutch, French, and English — which witnessed the dispersal of their neighboring kinsmen, the Huron and others. Several French priests were martyred for their faith (the North American Martyrs: see page 20) but their deaths could be

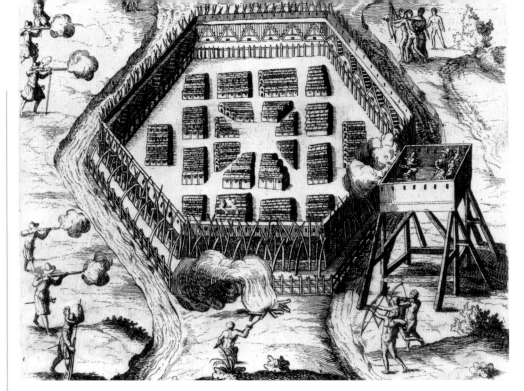

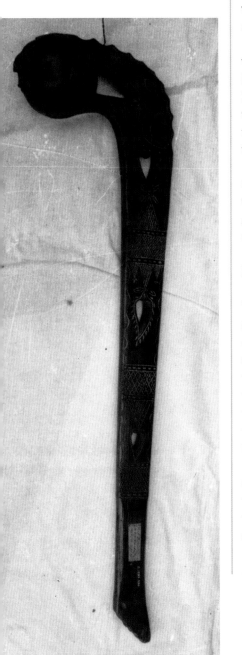

viewed as executions in order to rid themselves of sorcerers, which could be interpreted as not a barbarious deed but undertaken in accordance with their traditional legal procedures.

Before the iron trade pipe-tomahawks came into use among the Iroquois, their principal weapons were the bow, the stone-headed tomahawk, and the war club. The war club was a heavy weapon, usually made of ironwood with a large ball or knot at the end. It was about 2 feet in length and the ball 5 to 6 inches in diameter. It was held in the belt and used with terrible effect in close combat and was also thrown at distant objects. Beginning about 1630 these were gradually replaced with iron hatchets and guns, and body armor — wooden rods fastened together with thongs — became obsolete.

The range of Iroquois war parties was huge. They were at war with the Cherokee and Catawba in the south and with the Illinois and Sioux in the west. The last time the Iroquois were involved with war as a nation was the War of 1812, but individuals served in the American Civil War and both world wars: the Iroquois independently declared war on Germany, and considered World War II merely an extension of the Great War.

## FOOD AND FLORA

The Iroquois depended to a large extent on the staple food of corn (maize), beans, and squashes, called the "Three Sisters" or "supporters of life." Corn agriculture had reached eastern North America from the south or west perhaps 2,000 years ago and the agricultural activities were the center of their social and ceremonial life. According to some authorities they had up to 17 varieties of maize, 60 varieties of beans and eight native squashes. Besides the cultivated plants, women gathered many kinds of wild foods such as nuts, berries, roots, fruits, and fungi. Among these were strawberries, blackberries, blueberries, cranberries, turnips, plums, and grapes. There were numerous ways of preparing corn, among them hominy and samp — both produced from the dehulled kernels of maize — which were boiled with the addition of beans, nuts, or game. Soups were made from green corn, sometimes with the addition of beans, maple syrup, or sunflower seed. Puddings and bread were boiled or baked in ashes with additional ingredients. The hunter or warrior on the trail could subsist on small amounts of a mixture of ground corn meal and sugar, carried in a pouch.

Fishing was a pursuit of spring and summer and was done with weighted nets, weirs, and bone hooks. Maple sap, with its first harvest in early spring, was made into syrup

**Right:** Native Americans in traditional dress, including one man at the back dressed in a suit with a star badge, posed near a structure with sign "Six Nations Long House" at the Pan-American Exposition, Buffalo, NY. This World's Fair, held in 1901, is most notable for being the location of the assassination of President William McKinley.

**Below:** Jesse Cornplanter, Seneca ceremonialist, giving the address of welcome to Joseph Keppler, Rochester, NY, in 1937.

**Below right:** Jerry Aaron, Iroquois, Ontario, Canada, c. 1907.

and sugar. Hunting for meat was undertaken by family groups between harvest time and mid-winter, and the bones of bison, deer, elk, bear, raccoon, porcupine, marten, and other animals have been recovered from archaeological sites. Game was taken by deadfalls and nooses, snares, nets, spears, bow and arrow, and blowguns. The Iroquois also used many plants known to have medicinal properties, employing them for ailments which resulted from their life-style. They were, however, subject to digestive disorders, rheumatism, pneumonia, and conjunctivitis. Senecas were still selling their herbal medicines to whites in the early 20th century. After about 1620 European farm animals — including horses — were gradually adopted and integrated into Iroquois culture. By the 19th century the Iroquois on many reserves had become farmers in the Euro-American mode but this, too, has disappeared as most Iroquois descendants are now part of a wage-earning economy.

In the days before European settlement Iroquoia was an almost continuous forest of beech, birch, elm, pine, hemlock, aspen, fir, spruce, and cedar. The area was forbidding but fruitful with blueberry, bilberry, strawberry, and other fruits growing wild. The rivers teemed with pike, eels, perch, sturgeon, and catfish.

## RELIGION AND RITUALS

Iroquois religious and ceremonial beliefs centered around the idea that all beings, animals, plant foods, and objects had spirit force, and this spirit power flowed through all nature called *otennota* glossed *orenda*. Analysis of prayers shows an Iroquois pantheon of three spirit orders: spirit forces on earth; a middle level of spirits above the earth; and an upper pantheon of forces controlling the universe. Prayers, rituals, and thanksgiving songs addressed to the spirit world run through these deities upward to the Creator, "He who holds the sky" (Hawenniyo). Some rituals were addressed directly to the Creator, others to earth-bound animals by the medicine societies. The principal religious festivals which conformed to the agricultural cycle, at least until recent times, have been well documented and are as follows:

### Midwinter or New Year Festival
Held in late January or February, starting five days after the new moon of midwinter, and managed by male officials, the festival's function was to renew the ceremonial associations, give thanks to the Creator and to all spirit forces on earth, above, and universal. The medicine societies (such as the False Faces) were active to cure ailments and hear dream revelations.

### Maple Festival
March, to give thanks to the maple spirits after the sap is collected.

### Sun Shooting
In spring to give thanks to the sun and to dislodge from the sun a frog which delays the onset of spring.

### Planting Festival or Seed Dance
In May to ask the Creator to bless seeds before planting.

### Strawberry Festival
In June to give thanks for the ripening of the first fruits.

### Thunder Ceremony
To bring rain.

Jim Crow, Seneca ceremonialist at the Cattarangus Reservation, NY, c. 1905.

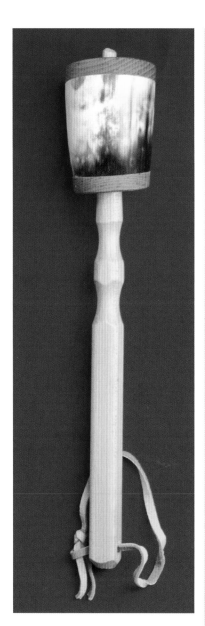

**Above:** Traditional cowhorn rattle used during ceremonial dances and songs.

**Opposite, top:** Iroquois dancers, singers, and drummers at Caledonia Park, Caledonia, Ontario, just off the Six Nations Indian Reserve, c. 1900. According to Jack Hayes the group includes George Key, George Smoke, James Beaver, Isaac Hill, and Andrew Spragg.

### Raspberry Harvest
In the middle of July.

### Green Bean Festival
In August to celebrate the ripening of the first cultivated crop.

### Small Green Corn Festival
In the second half of August.

### Big Green Corn Ceremonies
In late August to late September, to give thanks for all crops which have matured and repeats many rituals of the Midwinter Festival. Managed by men.

### Harvest Festival
In October to celebrate the storing of crops for winter; managed by women, thus completing the agricultural cycle.

In early times as many as 17 festivals have been reported, but today five or six are usually observed. The Midwinter and Big Green Corn solstice ceremonies are the major festivals at which the four sacred rituals are performed that return thanks to the Creator for the "Three Sisters our life supporters" — maize (Indian Corn), beans, and squash. These rites are the Great Feather Dance, the Drum or Thanksgiving Dance, men's Individual or Personal Chant, and the Bowl Game. Their functions are given below:

| | | |
|---|---|---|
| **Great Feather Dance**<br>Thanks to the Creator. | **Stirring of Ashes**<br>Dream fulfillment. | **Women Planters**<br>Thanks for the vegetables. |
| **Thanksgiving Dance**<br>Thanks to the Creator. | **False Face Society**<br>To exorcise (cure) disease. | **Corn Dance**<br>Now a social dance. |
| **Individual or Personal Chant** (men)<br>Thanks to the Creator. | **Husk Face Society**<br>Messengers of the food spirits. | **Bowl Game**<br>Thanks to the Creator. |
| **Hand-in-Hand Dance** (Bean Dance). Now a social dance. | **Medicine Society** (Society of Medicine Men, "Idos")<br>Curing. | **Women's Shuffle Dances** (Harvest Dances)<br>Thanks to the food spirits. |
| **Striking-the-Stick (Pole) Dance**<br>To cure and to bring rain. | **Buffalo Dance** (Company of Mystic Animals)<br>Curing and dream fulfillment. | **Stomp Dance**<br>Now a social dance. |

The Medicine societies may meet three or four times a year. Of these the Society of False Faces is the most famous. Their members wear facially distorted wooden carved masks for curing, followed by the Husk Face Society who connect with the food spirits, and the secret Society of Medicine Men. Other societies such as the Little Water, Little People, and Company of Mystic Animals are in reality orders of the Society of Medicine Men.

These thanksgiving ceremonies which continue today with slight variations at different longhouses are much the same as reported by Lewis Henry Morgan in 1851, the first white man to study Iroquois culture in depth. The rituals are those accepted by Handsome Lake,

the religious reformer at the beginning of the 19th century. He did not challenge the old faith, respecting the pantheon of spirit forces and annual calendrical festivals, but he revitalized the old system by adding a strict moral code he devised from Quaker influences, being preoccupied with confession and the elimination of social ills such as witchcraft and alcohol abuse. The emphasis of many rituals changed from success in the hunt or warfare to a curative content. However, the attention to dreams and concern for crops remains as reported in the *Relations des jésuites* of the 17th century. The code of Handsome Lake the prophet is preached in shortened form at the Midwinter and Big Green Corn Festivals, but the entire code is recited by professional speakers at various longhouses usually in the fall of alternating years. Fluent native speakers are now rare.

While the events take place in the longhouses or homes of the faithful, other events include sporadic seasonal rites, private medicine dances, public shows, and tribal or Six Nations' meetings, most of which take place in the longhouses, but they are independent of the calendrical ceremonies. Political meetings in the form of conventions of delegates from all longhouses in Canada and the United States also take place at regular intervals.

**Below:** Dancers from the Mohawk Nation at Caughnawaga (Kahnawana) who performed during a lacrosse tournament in the presence of HRH Prince Arthur, son of Queen Victoria, c. 1869.

**Above, from left to right:**
Six Nations Powwow July 2004.
Contemporary Pan-Indianism
arrived in southeastern Ontario in
the late 1970s. Male and female
dance regalia, singing, and dancing
based upon western Indian
celebrations are now held on most
Iroquois reserves.

The Sweetgrass Singers, female
singers from Caughnawaga
Mohawk (Kahnawake) Reserve,
Quebec, performing at the Iroquois
Museum, Howes Cave, NY, July
1998.

Six Nations Powwow,
contemporary Pan-Indian
celebration held at Six Nations
Reserve, Ontario, July 2004.

**Left:** Group portrait of St. Regis
Mohawk men and women in
costume outside log building, some
on horseback, 1894.

# Chapter 3: Material Culture

## INTRODUCTION

The Iroquois produced a wide variety of tools, utensils, and ornaments in wood, bark, antler, and stone. Before trade goods became available, they made stone arrowpoints, flint knives, and wedge-shaped hatchet heads, adzes, hammers, and mauls. From bone and antler were made awls, chisels, and other tools, needles, and fishing and hunting equipment, also bone beads, pendants, and combs. To prepare corn, it was crushed by means of a long-handled double-ended wooden pestle and upright mortar fashioned from a fire-hollowed log (see photograph on page 49). Other utensils connected with food were elm-bark containers and bowls, wooden bowls, cups, spoons, ladles, and stirrers. Iroquois pottery was more or less globular — a smooth body, round base, constricted neck with the outward flared collared rim bearing the major share of decoration. Later, during the historic period, notched rims were made. Decoration of pottery consisted of incised lines, angular designs, and chevron and triangle combinations. No use was made of painting on pottery, nor were there handles, but sometimes effigies of the human face appear. While women were the potters, men made excellent smoking pipes of clay or stone with effigies of animals or birds and humans.

Pre-contact Iroquois jewelry consisted of necklaces of bone beads, drilled teeth of bear, wolf, dog, lynx, elk, and other animals. With the dawn of the historic period, many new materials were adopted from European sources including glass beads, copper, brass, and silver ornaments including earrings, bracelets, and breast ornaments. Weapons in early times comprised the bow and arrow, war club headed with a wooden ball or antler prong, wooden or bark shield, and body armor of rods fastened together with thongs. Beginning about 1620 these weapons were gradually replaced with guns, iron hatchets, culminating in the pipe-tomahawk of the latter colonial period. Little is known of early Iroquois decorative arts beyond the designs used in pottery and on bone and antler articles. It is probable the embroidery techniques in quills and hair to be found on articles of clothing and bags used designs that were predominantly geometric and curvilinear that fit into the general historic art pattern of the whole Northeast. Realistic plant and floral representations, so common in later beadwork, are of European inspiration. The Iroquois also excelled in silverwork with head bands, bracelets, and earrings, originally obtained in trade, and later produced by their own craftsmen often using Scottish and Freemasonary designs. Real silver was replaced by German silver during the 19th century.

Ribbonwork was also developed, although it was not as important as among the southern

**Right:** Carved spoons and ladles, cherished property used for eating food in longhouse festivals. Iroquois, 19th century.

**Below right:** Iroquois corn husk doll in the form of a male singer sitting astride a wooden bench as might be seen in a longhouse ritual. The ceremonalist representation wears a buckskin kilt, braided wool sashes, moccasins, and roach. He holds a bark rattle. A carved miniature is attached to the bench. His tin arm and head bands represent silver adornments. Made c. 1950, measurements are 3.5 inches x 8 inches (89 mm x 203 mm).

**Opposite, top:** Iroquois splint-ash basket, two elm or hickory bark rattles, turtle shell rattle, wooden carved False Face mask with horsehair, and a 19th-century pouch with floral beadwork.

**Opposite, below:** Woven belt of Indian hemp, with the warps braided to form the tying straps. The central portion is twinned with false moosehair embroidery and edged with large white beads. Probably Iroquois, c. 1770. Collected by Sir John Caldwell, Canadian Museum of Civilization, Gatineau, Quebec.

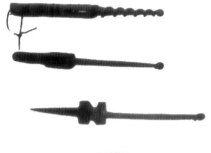

**Above:** Water drum and drum beaters, Schoharie Museum, N.Y.

**Opposite, top:** Burden straps or trumplines often worn across the forehead supporting a load carried on the back. Natural fibers and decorated with moosehair using a technique known as false embroidery. Similar straps are thought to be prisoner halters but narrower. Iroquois, 18th century.

**Opposite, below:** Woven wool, yarn or fiber garters with interspersed white beads. Probably Iroquois, late 18th/early 19th centuries.

**Below:** An Iroquois elm bark canoe and paddles — a drawing of an item collected by Lewis Henry Morgan and presented to the University of the State of New York, Albany, 1851, since destroyed by fire in 1911.

woodland peoples. Sometime during the late 17th or early 18th centuries the Iroquois appear to have adopted splint wood (ash or elm) basketry from the coastal Algonkian tribes: it remains a major craft industry today.

As early as 1634 European explorers reported that the exterior doors of the traditional Iroquois longhouse had iron hinges, and iron chains, bolts, hoopiron, and metal spikes were in use. The Jesuit, Isaac Jogues, reported in 1643 they were armed with guns. So it should be appreciated that all craftwork and artwork since the mid-17th century has been subject to European influences and technology.

Iroquois made canoes of elm and oak bark stitched to a frame of ash or hickory with basswood fiber, with strips of ash serving as ribs across the bottom of the canoe. No full-size Iroquois bark canoe has survived. They also made dugout canoes from logs reduced to the desired length by fire and hollowed out by a further process of charring and scraping. They made woven burden straps from various natural fibers. These were used as tumplines for carrying cradleboards, wood, or heavy baskets on their backs.

The Iroquois also produced prisoner ties with geometrical designs using a technique called "false embroidery." Native fiber or later wool sashes and garters had interspaced beads, and moccasins had their instep covered with quillwork and ankle flaps with quillwork, beadwork, or ribbonwork. Early pouches and other objects often had tin-cone fringes with deer hair added along the edges to give sounds that emphasized movement.

Cradleboards were made from flat boards approximately 18 inches wide and 24 inches long (45.7 cm x 61 cm) with a protruding bow near the top and a foot-board at the bottom. Cradle boards dating from about 1830 were often painted and carved with floral designs especially by the St. Regis Mohawks. Babies were held by broadcloth embroidered with beads and silver ornaments with buckskin bands to hold the baby in place.

The Iroquois had several different methods of making baskets. Simple checkered plaiting, over and under, of black ash splints, then more complex plaiting including twisting to produce a series of pointed scrolls or curves. Demand from whites for baskets included sewing baskets, laundry hampers, and recently decorative examples painted or stamped with designs produced by a wood block or a potato cut in half with a design cut in relief dipped in dye and applied to the wider splints of the baskets. Snowshoes were used both while hunting and in warfare, and were necessary for almost one-third of the year. They were built on a frame of hickory with two or more crossbraces and filled with a netting of sinew or skin thongs (rawhide or babiche).

Of the Iroquois' games, lacrosse is perhaps the best-known. Today, it is the Iroquois' national game with teams occasionally touring overseas. Indeed, the Iroquois Nationals, the national men's team, was admitted to the world body, the International Lacrosse Federation in 1990, the only such team involved in international sports. They have proved extremely successful, having been runners-up in all three World Indoor championships (2003, 2007,

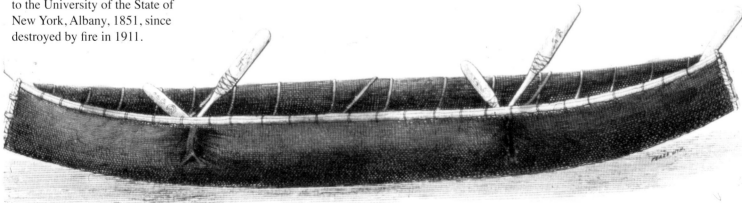

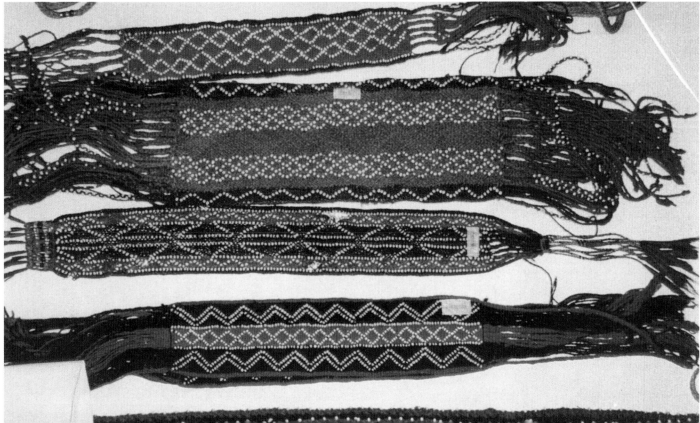

**Above:** Black-dyed buckskin pouches with porcupine quillwork decoration; late 18th century, probably Iroquois.

**Above right:** Bag with strap, decorated with imitation glass wampum and quillwork. Probably Huron but Iroquoian type, 18th century. Thunderbird and Lightning Exhibition, Museum of Mankind, British Museum, 1982.

**Far right:** Lacrosse racket. Schoharie Museum, NY.

**Below:** Iroquois carved effigy pipe, early 18th century.

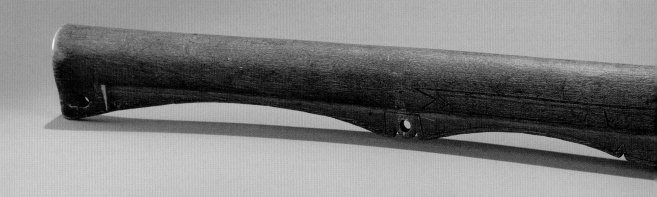

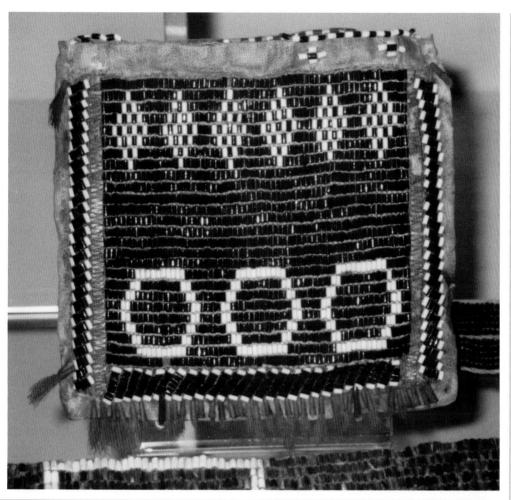

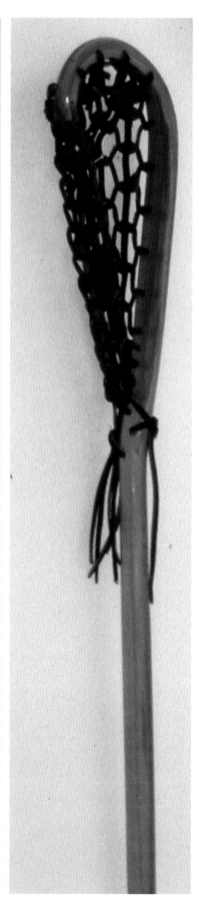

2011) and fourth in the three men's field hockey tournaments it has attended (1998, 2002, 2006). The women's team, the Haudenosaunee Nation, became a member in 2008. Lacrosse is a ball game played between two teams and can be played indoors (box lacrosse) or out (field lacrosse). The objective — to drive the ball through the opposing goal — requires lacrosse rackets for each player, a curved stick with a net — before modern materials, the Iroquois used babiche — to catch the ball.

The Snow Snake game had smooth flexible metal-tipped rods made from maple, walnut, or hickory. These were thrown along a packed snow course with victory for the greatest distance thrown. Similar sticks, poles, and spears were made for hoop games.

The traditional Iroquois drum was the so-called water drum, a hollowed out log or whiteman's tub. Over the top, a tightly stretched skin was held in place by an encircling thong or rope. Drumsticks were small and sometimes ornately carved.

Rattles of elm, or hickory bark folded over, with a wooden handle, used peach or cherry stones for the sound. Large turtleshell rattles were only used for religious ceremonies.

Corn husk was used to produce dolls and masks for members of the Husk Face Society either braided or twined.

Carved wooden masks for the False Face Society were usually carried out by artists of exceptional ability, and carved from the trunk of a living basswood, willow, or other softwood trees in order to retain the potency and spirit of the tree. The masks were often painted black or red, and have tin-plate eyes and horse hair wigs.

**Above:** Iroquois-type cradleboard, Schoharie Museum, NY.

**Right:** Rear view of a Mohawk cradleboard, c. 1840. About this time the Mohawks of St. Regis and Caughnawaga began to carve and paint the wooden backs of their cradleboards with elaborate floral, bird and animal designs.

**Far right:** Rear view of a painted Mohawk cradleboard, c. 1930.

**Opposite:** Mrs. Marquis, Kahnawake Mohawk, c. 1890. Her daughter in a cradleboard was named Kwanentawi.

**Right:** St. Regis Indians transporting baskets to the trading post.

**Opposite, below:** St. Regis Indian Trading Company basket catalog of c.1900 with contemporary period ash-splint baskets with original tags.

**Below:** Iroquois woodsplint basket with potato stamp designs from Ontario, Canada, c.1900.

## WOODSPLINT BASKETS

Baskets made from strips of shaved down ash or oak (sometimes of other woods) and simply woven were originally made as utilitarian work baskets for gathering and storing wood, for household and market use. Many large older baskets have elaborately carved handles. In more recent times small decorative baskets were made for sale to museums, collectors, and tourists. However, it is possible Indian people adopted the plaited woodsplint technique from European settlers in Northeastern America during the 18th century where baskets may be confused with immigrant basketry particularly of the Shakers, Pennsylvania-Germans, and Swedish peoples. Northeastern Indians (Iroquois, Mohegans, and Scaticooks) sometimes added painted, swabbed, or stencilled designs.

By the latter part of the 1800s, large numbers of baskets were being sold to tourists at such places as Saratoga Springs or Niagara Falls. Basketry at the St. Regis (now Akwesasne) Reservation, in particular, grew because of the St. Regis trading post. The St. Regis Indian Trading Company was set up to sell its goods countrywide.

Woodsplint basket-making is a labor-intensive process that starts with felling a suitable black ash tree before stripping the bark. The log then has to be split into long narrow splints by means of a steel knife or gauge before weaving. This (**Above and Right**) large circular plaited woodsplint basket was made c. 1900. It is 15 inches in diameter and 7 inches deep (38 cm x 17.8 cm) with pointed protrusions (Union flags?). The narrow weft splints are interwoven with the wider warp splints. This type of basket with solid handles was typically by Iroquois from Southern Ontario.

**Above and Left:** Circular painted woodsplint and sweetgrass basket, Iroquois c. 1920. The splints were originally dyed green, blue, and purple although now faded. Many of this type were marketed commercially and sold throughout the northeast and many came from the St. Regis Reservation. It is of 11-inch (28 cm) diameter.

**Above and Right:** This Iroquois large rectangular carrying basket, for gathering or storing food, is dated c. 1900. With wide woodsplints simply woven, and two finely carved solid handles, it is 18 inches long, 13 inches wide, and 6.5 inches deep (46 cm x 33 cm x 16.5 cm).

**Opposite, above:** A group of Akwesasne Mohawk fancy strawberry baskets, early and late 20th century. Akwesasne means "where the partridge drums."

**Opposite, below:** Splint-ash baskets, Iroquois market, Roberson Center, Binghamton, NY, 1987.

**Above:** Tree bark roofing.

**Opposite, above:** Iroquois longhouse shelter. Pitched-roof bark longhouse reconstruction, with entrance and vestibule for storing wood. External vertical posts shown.

**Opposite, below:** Typical Iroquois village with old curved-roof longhouses, and showing women drying and preparing corn.

**Below:** Interior view of a longhouse showing family compartments.

## LONGHOUSES

Iroquois dwellings, both single and communal, followed a basic plan and were arranged in villages with as many as 120 lodges, or in hamlets with as few as four or five bark lodges. They ranged in size from, perhaps, a maximum of 150 feet (45.5 m) long, 25 feet (7.6 m) in breadth, and 20 feet (6 m) high for communal longhouses to small family houses of about 20 feet (6 m) long, 15 feet (4.5 m) wide, and the same height. The longhouses were constructed with elm, ash, or basswood bark sheets usually removed from trees in spring. These were fixed to upright posts some four or five feet apart and roof supports bent in an arch shape, all tied together with inner bark strips or twisted cords. Overlapping roof bark slabs were vertically affixed with the sides "shingled" horizontally. These sheets of bark were held securely between the inner frame posts and smaller poles placed lengthwise on the roof and upright along the walls.

The earliest European reports of longhouses identified curved roofs but later pitched profiles were also used. Smoke holes were left at intervals in the roof, and at either end shed-like vestibules allowed storing of wood and food. From the rafters hung bunches of corn braided together by the husks and other dried foods. Inside the longhouse was a corridor with compartments on either side. These were sectioned off with bark for, perhaps, two families sharing opposite living compartments. This form of longhouse endured until about the end of the 18th century, when one-family, square-shaped log cabins of the type introduced to the frontier by Europeans were adopted. Such homes are still seen on a number of present-day reservations. Since the early 19th century the description "longhouse" refers to a large community building made of logs and nowadays covered with clapperboard shingles. They are used for Iroquois religious, social, and political meetings and found on several reservations. These long rectangular buildings have two stoves (equivalent to hearths in old bark lodges) near each end, and rows of benches line each side where the two moieties — Wolf or Deer (Turtle) — face each other. In the center is a bench for

**Below right:** The Coldspring Longhouse, Steamburg, Allegany-Seneca Reservation, NY. This longhouse was built to replace the old one when the Kinzua Dam was opened in 1965 flooding the area, including the old Cornplanter grant across the border in Pennsylvania.

**Opposite, top:** Longhouses at Six Nations Reserve, Ontario, photographed 1990. The Lower Cayuga Longhouse with the cookhouse and dining-hall-kitchen to the left, where large cauldrons of meat and soups are cooked over an open fire. There are two Cayuga longhouses at Six Nations, the Lower Cayuga and Upper Cayuga or Sour Springs Longhouse. Both have congregations noted for their conservatism and elements of Delaware ritual influence.

**Opposite, center:** The Seneca Longhouse with the dining-hall-kitchen beyond. Behind both is the old cookhouse. This longhouse was built in 1881.

**Below:** The Onondaga Longhouse, with the old cookhouse and dining hall behind. This century-old frame longhouse was replaced with a new log structure in 1991.

singers and drummers, around which an open area or path allows dancing and rituals to take place. Sometimes the whole of Iroquoia was viewed symbolically as a longhouse of one family. Similarly, a series of metaphors regarding the longhouse, its site, fires, central corridor, etc., were applied to their ancient territory.

The present-day longhouses and the reservations are as follows:
Coldspring or Steamburg (Allegany), Newton (Cattaraugus), Tonawanda (Tonawanda), Onondaga (Onondaga), St. Regis (Akwesasne) all in New York; Sour Springs, Seneca, Onondaga and Lower Cayuga (Six Nations Reserve) and Oneida (Oneida of the Thames) all in Ontario; Caughnawaga (Kahnawake) in Quebec; and Seneca-Cayuga in Oklahoma.

**Left:** An old log cabin, one of the few homes constructed like this remaining on the Tonawanda Reservation, NY.

**Right:** Young woman wearing an Iroquois Glengarry hat and moccasins decorated with raised embossed floral beadwork of the 1860 era. Her purse may also be Iroquois.

**Color Plates (pages 78–79)**

**18th-Century Warriors (page 78)**
**Left:** This warrior has roached hair, a painted face, and his arms and legs are tattooed. He wears silver earrings, a tradecloth blanket with ribbon appliqué, red tradecloth leggings with knee garters, and holds a flintlock. His dress is the merger of European traded materials with native attire.

**Center:** With a headdress of traded ostrich feathers, a fiber-woven belt sash with interspaced beads, blue tradecloth leggings with garters, and buckskin moccasins, this warrior holds a ball-headed war club. By the 18th century indigenous materials of animal skins had been partly replaced by trade goods for dress.

**Right:** This warrior has a small roach worn on the back of his head, and wears a neck knife case, silver armbands, a belt pouch, a tradecloth breechclout, and black-dyed buckskin leggings with quillwork and garters. His moccasins are decorated with quillwork, and his tradecloth blanket is a replacement for a fur robe of a previous era.

**Background:** Two lacrosse players (left); Fort Niagara (right), scene of the Iroquois-aided victory for the British in 1759 during the French and Indian War.

**19th-Century Iroquois (page 79)**
**Left:** This Iroquois man holds a Condolence Cane, which records pictographically the names of the 50 hereditary chiefs of the League of the original Five Nations. It

# DRESS

As clothing was highly perishable, no examples of early Iroquois clothing have survived. The likelihood is that clothing was originally buckskin — chiefly deer — tanned soft with animal brains after dehairing. Gradually, garments of skin were replaced by trade-cloth and Iroquois women became expert with needle, thread, and scissors by the mid-18th century. The most sought-after cloths were English strouds, which were lighter than furs and animal skins, easier to dry, and so more suitable for mobile life in the forests. The cloth also came in bright colors: blue, red, black, and green. Typical Iroquois traditional dress for both sexes was, therefore, a harmonious blend of native and European materials, design, and decoration.

Iroquois women wore a skirt of broadcloth patterned after the old buckskin skirt which was left open to the knee on the right side. The border and corner of the left hand side were decorated with beadwork or ribbonwork. Leggings of buckskin or cloth were secured with ties below the knees. Leggings were made with the seams at the front left open about four inches above the foot to allow the leggings to fit over the moccasins. Leggings were also decorated similar to skirt borders. Women also wore traded skirts, gaiters, and overdresses often covered with silver brooches of various shapes. Later these garments were made by the Iroquois women themselves.

Women's moccasins — like those of the men — were of various types. The most important and no doubt the oldest form was the one piece of buckskin construction with a center-seam over the instep and a heel seam. These moccasins had a collar or ankle flap, a buckskin extension to the top edge, which was folded down and often decorated with quillwork, moosehair, or beadwork. Later a second form became universally popular among all woodland tribes which used a "U"-shaped vamp over the instep with heavy puckering to the top unit and an inverted "T"-shaped heel seam (and other variations).

Iroquois women took pride in their long, shining black hair, well pomaded with sunflower oil. All parted their hair in the center; mothers drew their hair back into a single braid.

The dress of men originally consisted of a breechclout, a fur robe or a deerskin shirt of two skins joined at the upper corners, deerskin kilt, leggings, and moccasins. Warrior's hair was scorched off and plucked out of the head; face, body, and limbs were tattooed, ears slit and nose bored to be adorned with silver rings. Later they wore colonial hunting coats, either skin or trade cloth, tube leggings or with front seams, and moccasins similar to those of their women, decorated with quillwork, moosehair, or beadwork. Later moccasins had velvet and broadcloth vamps and cuffs. Men wore woven sashes, originally of native fibers but later of woven yarn, and silver ornaments obtained in trade, or made by their own silversmiths, but often in designs of European origin. Imported beads were supplied to Iroquois as early as 1610 and gradually beadwork replaced porcupine quillwork and thread replaced sinew. Traditional designs of natural and geometric forms were replaced by floral designs particularly in the 19th century. Shell wampum beads were also used for personal adornments. During the latter part of the 18th century silk ribbons were also used to decorate Iroquois clothing.

Iroquois men of importance wore a headdress called gustoweh, made on a frame of splints which arched over the head with a silver or beaded band and a feather which revolved in a tube fixed to a frame. For many years traditional dress for both male and female was rarely seen, but it has made a significant revival in recent times. With the spread of Pan-Indianism in the 20th century both western Indian dress and dance costumes have also been adopted for Powwows.

was used as an aid to memory in the long recital of the Condolence Ceremony when new chiefs were installed. He wears crossed bandolier bags with Iroquoian beaded double-curve and floralistic motifs typical of the first half of the 19th century. He has examples of silverwork — which came to the Iroquois from Montreal silversmiths and which the Indians copied — on his gustoweh headdress, earrings, and nose ring. He also wears buckskin moccasins with ankle collars.

**Center:** Kahnawake (Caughnawaga) mother and child c. 1890. Several native troops from this reserve gave public performances in Canada, the United States, and Europe. Lavish, large-bead embossed floral designs embellished the dress of women, men, and children, as shown here on her crown, skirt, and strips. She also has numerous metal German silver brooches. The child is held in a wooden-backed cradle with protective bow in front.

**Right:** Six Nations Chief of the mid-19th century. He wears a feather headdress with a band and brooches of — perhaps — silver (later they would have been of German silver). Around his waist he wears a braided wool sash (earlier examples were of native fibers) with interspaced beads. He has black-dyed skin leggings finely decorated with beadwork and ribbonwork.

**Background:** A traditional elm bark longhouse with the extended posts and rafters. One entrance is shown (there was usually one at each end at east and west). Modern clapperboard longhouses are meeting places and still used for rituals.

**Inset:** An Ojibwa lady wears an 1860s-style Oneida outfit consisting of a beaded headdress, tunic, skirt, and moccasins. She holds a large splint-ash basket. The Ojibwa lady modeling the dress is Naomi Smith of Chippewas of Nawash, Saugeen Peninsula, Ontario.

**Iroquois of the 20th/21st Century (page 80)**

**Left:** Elder wearing a headdress with a metal band and a cloth blanket. The beadwork on his cloth coat and leggings shows the revival of traditional designs. The double-curve motif is a series of repeating inward or outward-facing beadwork designs (once executed in porcupine quillwork) shown here around the bottom edge of his coat and leggings.

**Center:** Iroquois lady dressed for a contemporary celebration based upon traditional costume. She wears a Glengarry cap, side-fold skirt, open-front leggings, vamp moccasins, and metal brooches on her collar. She holds a fringed dance-shawl and wears a beaded bandolier bag.

**Right:** Pan-Indian powwows were first held on the First Nations Reserves of southern Ontario during the 1970s and 1980s. This man wears a porcupine hair roach and eaglefeather bustle emblematic of the so-called "Traditional Dancer." At the Six Nations Reserve they hold the annual Champion of Champions Powwow in late July or August adjacent to the stately Chiefswood Museum. For many years the Mohawks at Six Nations held an annual pageant as well.

**Background:** The flag of the Haudenosaunee Confederacy showing the five constituent original member tribes represented by five linked figures, and (at right) a traditional longhouse with a modern solar panel.

**Left:** Mrs. Esther Phillips, a Mohawk of the Caughnawaga (Kahnawake) Reserve, Quebec, photographed in 1978 outside the Church of St. Francis-Xavier. She wears a western Pan-Indian costume her ancestors would not recognize.

**Right and Opposite**: Iroquois woman's dress, front and back, c. 1850. The lady wears a carefully reconstructed costume worn for festive occasions including a Glengarry cap, a cloth overdress with silver brooches, and a broadcloth skirt open to the knee on the right side. The border and corner of the skirt is beaded with sky dome and multiple diamond designs. She also wears a beaded bandolier bag, wampum, and bead necklaces.

**Above:** Young boy, probably Iroquois, wearing beaded belt, coat (or skirt) and headdress. Photographer Henry Eggman, Otterville, Ontario, c. 1870

**Right:** An eastern Indian in full regalia, c. 1860. He is probably an Iroquois. Note the beaded crown of his headdress and pouch which appears to be a bandolier of heart-shaped rosettes.

**Left:** Charles Johnson, Seneca ceremonialist at the Tonawanda Reservation, NY, c. 1900. He wears a sash, armbands, leggings, and moccasins in typical traditional Iroquois style.

**Top:** Iroquois Indians c. 1890, possibly part of a troupe or traveling show.

**Above:** Group of Mohawks probably from Caughnawaga (Kahnawake) Reserve, near Montreal, Quebec, c. 1880. They all wear fine beaded capes or collars with floral, bird and flag designs.

**Right:** Iroquois moccasins of black-dyed buckskin with collars and vamp decorated with beadwork, c. 1850.

**Below:** Iroquois moccasins of c. 1860 made from commercial leather and red cloth decorated with beadwork including the popular configuration of an eight-lobed design element.

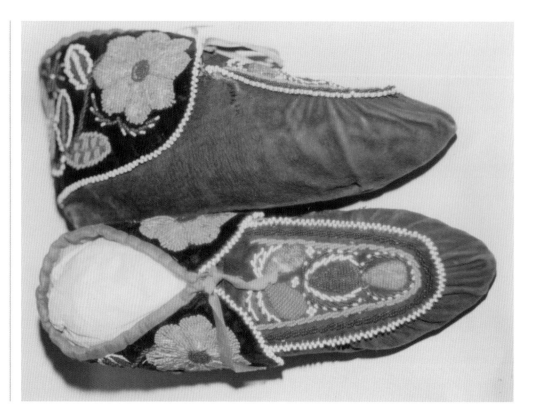

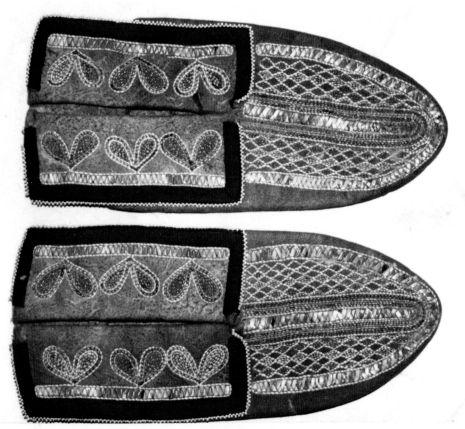

**Left:** Iroquois moccasins, early 19th century. Buckskin decorated with porcupine quillwork.

**Below left:** Moccasins, probably c. 1910 Kahnawake (Caughnawaga) Mohawk, made from commercial leather, cloth, velvet and using large size beads.

**Below:** Early 19th century style Iroquois moccasins made from buckskin with beadwork and ribbon-trimmed ankle flaps.

**Right:** Iroquois buckskin moccasins from the early 19th century. Both cuffs and instep are decorated with porcupine quillwork.

**Opposite:** A pair of early 19th century buckskin Iroquois moccasins, probably Seneca. The fronts are decorated with porcupine quillwork and the red trade cloth collars are beaded and edged with silk.

**Below:** Iroquois buckskin moccasins, early 19th century. Left and center, buckskin with quillwork; right, buckskin with cloth collars and beadwork.

**Above and Right:** Quillwork on a black buckskin robe from the Eastern Great Lakes (possibly Iroquois) decorated in zoomorphic and anthropomorphic designs; late 18th century.

**Opposite:** Buckskin coat with beadwork and a dark cloth bandolier shoulder bag also decorated with beadwork. Probably Iroquois, early 19th century, today on show at the Horniman Museum, London, England.

**Above:** Chiefs of the Six Nations at Brantford, Canada, explaining their wampum belts to Horatio Hale, September 14, 1871. Image shows Joseph Snow (Hahriron), Onondaga chief; George H. M. Johnson (Deyonhehgon), Mohawk chief, government interpreter, and son of John "Smoke" Johnson; John Buck (Skanawatih), Onondaga chief, hereditary keeper of the wampum; John "Smoke" Johnson (Sakayenkwaraton), Mohawk chief, speaker of the council; Isaac Hill (Kawenenseronton), Onondaga chief, fire keeper; John Seneca Johnson (Kanonkeredawih), Seneca chief. Hale said, "The wampum belts were explained to me on the reserve, at the residence of Chief G. H. M. Johnson; and at my request the chiefs afterwards came with me to Brantford, where the original photograph ... was taken."

**Right:** Richard Hamell and his reproduction of the "Two Dog Wampum Belt." According to oral tradition, this wampum belt was made when some Mohawks joined the Algonkins and Nipissings at Oka, Quebec (Lake of Two Mountains or Kaneshsatake) from Montreal Island in 1721. The white line shows the length of their lands, the eight figures with clasped hands are groups loyal to French Catholic priests represented by the central cross, and the dogs (one for each end) guarding the boundaries of their lands. The eight figures probably represent the French plus the Seven Nations of Canada loyal to French Canada until the close of the French and Indian War in 1760.

## WAMPUM

The term wampum comes from an Algonkian word *wampumpeak*, meaning strings of white shell beads. Wampum were 0.25-inch (6 mm) long cylindrical shell beads usually made in two colors. White wampum was made principally from the central column of the whelk; purple wampum (often called black) was obtained from the quahog clam. These shells were found along the Atlantic coast, particularly in Long Island Sound. Purple wampum, being more difficult to make, was twice as valuable as white. Although native-made wampum pre-dates the European invasion of eastern North America, it was not until after the Europeans had brought steel awls and other implements that making wampum became highly developed and it was used as a medium of exchange.

During the 18th century European settlers in New Jersey took over wampum production, and French glass beads of similar shape and size were also used as a substitute for shell wampum. Wampum belts were beads woven using sinew, vegetable fiber, or in later ones, thread, to form a rectangular belt usually much longer than wide. Of the two colors, white was considered to symbolize peace or life, while black was said to symbolize war or death. Red paint and other pigments were sometimes added to the belt to signify war. Strings of wampum were used as credentials or certificates of authority for recording the Great Law, and identifying chiefs and matrons. In public debates strings or belts of wampum served to refresh the memory. Belts of woven wampum were given and received at treaty negotiations and ceremonies as seals of friendship, or as records, and might contain designs which symbolized the event. Such belts would then be used as mnemonic devices to recall the event it symbolized at future meetings. Wampum belts played a large role in conveying, accepting, or rejecting messages and proposals at treaties. During the late 19th and early 20th centuries important wampum belts were sold to collectors and museums from both the Six Nations in Canada and the New York Iroquois. Some have recently been returned. One of the most famous belts is the so-called "Hiawatha Belt," symbolizing the League's formation. It consists of four rectangles and a tree of peace linked by a path (lines). The five design elements represent the five original nations at the League's foundation.

**Below:** Wampum belts with woven (possibly shell) beads made to convey information about events, peaceful or warlike, between tribes or between Indians and whites. The middle belt has an attached turtle effigy, 18th century probably Iroquois or neighboring groups. Thunderbird and Lightning Exhibition, Museum of Mankind, 1982.

**Right:** Wampum belt, tribe unknown but possibly an Iroquois type, c. 1780. Woven in French glass imitation wampum beads. The design shows groups of humans holding hands, probably indicating friendship or alliance. The use of dark-color background suggests probable alliance in war. Collected by Arent Schuyler de Peyster, a British commandant at Michilimackinac 1774–1779 and today on show at the National Museums & Galleries on Merseyside, Liverpool, England.

**Top right:** Wampum belt of purple and white shell beads, c. 1770, tribe unknown, possibly Iroquois. Collected by Sir John Caldwell (Fifth baronet, Castle Caldwell, Fermanagh, Ireland) when an ensign at Fort Niagara or adjutant at Fort Detroit, between 1774 and 1780. Today on show at the Canadian Museum of Civilization, Gatineau, Quebec.

**Far right:** The 24 Nations Belt or Annual Presents Belt held by Richard D. Hamell.

**Center right:** The Wyandot Two Row Belt of 1748. There is no known image of the original belt. This reconstruction by Richard D. Hamell is a hybrid of information from the Canadian Treaty Belt and others including Darren Bonaparte, Akwensasne Mohawk. The outline body at left is the Governor of New York; the five solid bodies are the Iroquois and the Wyandot, with the hatchet on the right. The two lines may represent the two "roads" between the nations.

**Bottom right:** Fort Niagara Treaty Belt of 1764 reproduced by Richard D. Hamell.

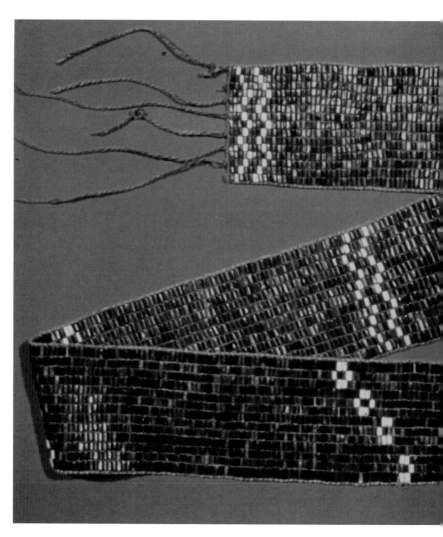

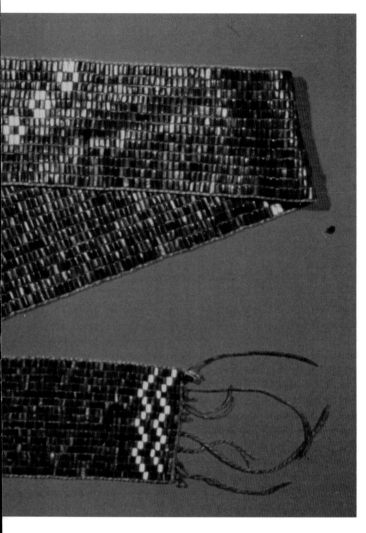

**1 CROOKED FACE MASK**
These doctor masks represent
Hadui (Seneca), Hadowi (Onondaga), or Atoweh (Mohawk), the
"Great Doctor" or "World Rim
Dweller," a prototype man-being
whose face became disfigured
during a fight with the Creator.
The myth has many varitions, but
briefly: the Creator met a stranger
(some say his twin brother). They
argued and during a fight the World
Rim Dweller struck a mountain,
breaking his nose, and his mouth
distorting with pain. Realizing he
had great power, the Creator
assigned the World Rim Dweller
the task of doctoring the sick. In
return, he requested humans make
wooden portrait masks of the
World Rim Dweller and to feed
them with tobacco and corn mush
when not in use. Such masks are
popularly called crooked mouth
or wry-mouth masks. Many come
from Grand River Reserve.

**2 DOCTOR MASK** with straight
lips. While masked Doctors hop,
crawl, and blow ashes on patients
to frighten away disease, Doorkeepers, often wearing straight-
lipped masks, stand upright in
doorways of homes or longhouses
to bar exit or entrance while rituals
are in progress.

**3 SPOON-LIPPED MASK** sometimes with tongue. A Doctor/Door-
keeper's mask, spoon-lipped masks
were common at Cattaraugus and
Allegany, sometimes paired in
doorkeeper rituals.

**MASKS**

Wooden masks with startlingly misshapen carved faces are among the most well-known
items of Iroquois material culture. Three distinct medicine societies employ masks. The first
are the False Face Company (Hondowitshera), who wear their masks in public or private to
perform their rituals at the Midwinter and Green Corn festivals for the exorcism of disease.
Some society members wear Doctor masks, others the Common Face and Beggar masks
who help Doctors to cure. Mask wearers crawl like cripples, or jump-hop, and through the
mouths of these masks hot ashes are blown (as a spirit force) or strewn over the floor or
rubbed on the hair and arms of the patients. Although there was local diversity in the ritual
and practices in the various Iroquois communities, wooden False Face masks represent
earth-bound supernatural forest beings who agree not to harm humans provided they
are given offerings of tobacco and corn mush. When masks are not in use, they must be
anointed periodically with sunflower oil. The custodians of Doctor masks (some called
Doorkeeper's masks) also anoint and address them with prayers.

The second society of mask wearers are the Husk Faces or Bushy-Heads, whose
membership is gained by a dream or curing dance. They represent another clan of earth-
bound supernatural beings who formed a pact with mankind and taught them the arts of
hunting and agriculture.

The third society to use masks were the Idos or Secret Society of Medicine Men, including
the Company of Mystic Animals. Dr. William Fenton, the leading authority on False Face
masks, has classified 12 types of masks based upon their face-mouth shape characteristics
(not their functions); many have tin-plate eyes and horse hair.

Of the types illustrated on this spread, generally types 1, 2 and 7 are doctor masks which
recall the mythological Great Doctor, whose face was distorted after a fight with his twin
brother (see story in 1). The remainder are Common Faces or Beggars, although 3 and 5 are
also associated with doctoring. Masks 2 and 3 are often Doorkeepers at Seneca longhouses,
while Doctors do their work. Masks 9 and 10 may also be called in to act as Doctors. The
Tuscaroras, in the main, did not share the mask-making complex of the other Iroquois tribes.
Similar masks were made by the Delaware but the Cherokee beggar masks are apparently
unrelated. During the late 19th and early 20th centuries many were sold to museums and
collectors. Recently, Iroquois have made efforts to reclaim them or to have access to them
to feed them ritually.

**4 HANGING MOUTH MASK**
sometimes Doctor masks, this old Seneca type is from Buffalo Creek, Onondaga, and Tonawanda.

**5 PROTRUDING TONGUE MASK**
often used by Beggars and Common Faces, this type of mask is uncommon outside the Onondaga.

**6 SMILING MASK** often used by Beggars, they could replace wry-faced masks, and were mostly used by the Seneca and Onondaga.

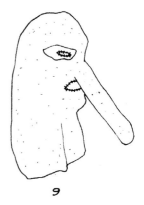

**7 WHISTLING MASK** with puckered lips and wrinkles, this is a class of beggar mask mostly used by the Seneca from Grand River Reserve.

**8 DIVIDED MASK** represents a spirit in half-human and half-supernatural form. Painted red and black, they were often used by Cayuga, Onondaga, Grand River, and Delaware.

**9 LONG-NOSED MASK** represents the trickster and is used to threaten naughty children. Usually made of cloth or buckskin, occasionally wood.

**10 HORNED OR BUFFALO MASK,** used by the medicine societies, these are rare and relatively recent. They are possibly caricatures of other races and gods.

**11 ANIMAL MASK** (various species) These rare masks are used by the medicine societies. Pig masks are a possible replacement for bear symbolism.

**12 BLIND MASK** without eyes: little is known about the origins of these masks, which are used by medicine societies.

## IROQUOIS & DELAWARE MASKS

**Top left:** Old teardrop-shaped wry-face mask. Red with black and white décor, tin eyes, three rim holes, bone teeth, and braided corn husk wig. Caughnawaga Mohawk.

**Top right:** Early spoonmouth, c. 1820, Tutelo, Grand River. Collected by Frank Speck. Brown with gray hair, brass eyes, tobacco bags, three rim holes.

**Center left:** Crooked face or wry-mouth. Often reproduced on maskettes. Oneida, brown with tin eyes, three rim hole.

**Center right:** Smiling mask. Brown, no metal eyes, racoons toupe. Oneida of the Thames, collected by Harrington.

**Bottom left:**Wry-face or crooked face Doctor mask, Rim of the World figure "Hadui." Red with tin eyes brown mouth, five rim holes. Mohawk, Grand River.

**Bottom right:** Wry-faced old "Hadui" mask. Brown with five rim holes, tin eyes. Mohawk, Grand River

.

**Top left:** Wry-mouth mask, orange and red with tin eyes and tobacco bag. Three rim holes. Mohawk, Grand River.

**Top right:** Common face on Delaware big-house posts. Natural wood; no tin or metal eyes. Oklahoma Delaware.

**Center left:** Whistling or ash-blower mask, red with black daubs; Oklahoma Delaware.

**Center right:** Protruding tongue mask, old type. Red with black wrinkles, tin eyes and four rim holes; Oklahoma Delaware.

**Bottom left:** Old spoon-lipped mask. Black with red mouth, tin eyes and five rim holes; Oklahoma Delaware.

**Bottom right:** Oneida. No information.

**Right:** Crooked face or "Hadui" mask, with twisted mouth, horsehair, and tinplate eyes.

**Opposite:** A crooked-face mask of c. 1940, made of wood with tinplate eyes and horsehair. Facially disfigured with a twisted mouth. Also a turtleshell rattle used in False Face rituals.

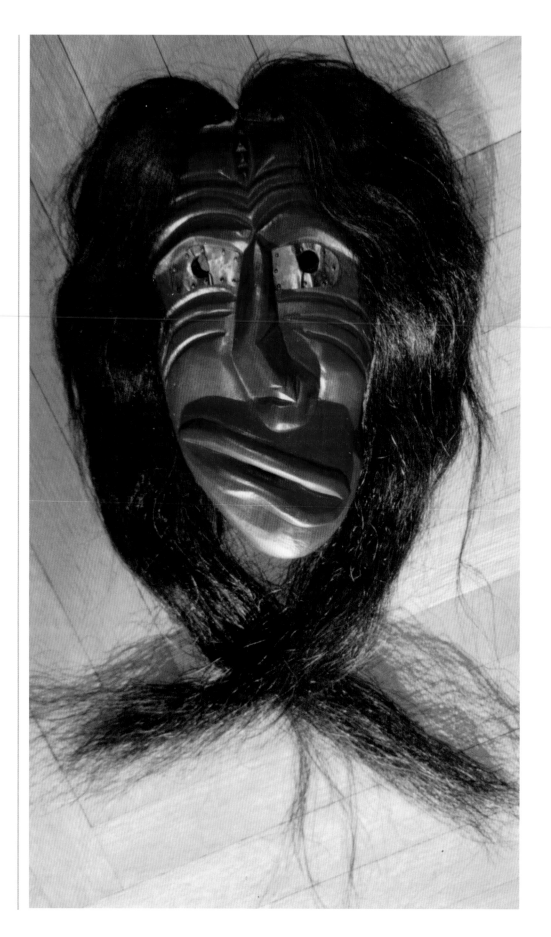

**Opposite:** A spoon-lipped shaped mask, from the Cattarangus Reservation, NY, with horsehair and metal eyes, c. 1900. Thunderbird and Lightning Exhibition, Museum of Mankind, London, 1982.

**Left:** Iroquois smiling mouth, c. 1900.

**Left:** Iroquois crafts of the 20th century: False Face mask; maskettes; cornhusk mask; turtleshell rattle. All formerly S. Cahoon Collection.

**Opposite:** Spoon-lipped Cayuga False Face Mask of the early 20th century; University of Philadelphia.

**Below:** Smiling-face Seneca False Face Mask; University of California.

Both masks are painted black and red with tinplate eyes.

**Opposite:** Yvonne Thomas, daughter of Jacob "Jake" Thomas, one of the last pre-eminent wooden mask carvers of Six Nations, Ontario. Yvonne — presently one of the last corn-husk craftworkers — runs the Jake Thomas Learning Center.

**Left and Above:** Corn-husk mask and maskette, as worn by members of the Husk Faces or Bushy-Heads Society.

**Below and Opposite:** Black buckskin tab pouch or belt pouch, Eastern Great Lakes, possibly Iroquois, late 18th century. Such bags have zoomorphic — beaver, turtle — and other images — thunderbird, celestial tree — in quill linework. One authority suggested the Iroquois should be ruled out as makers of such pouches since the iconography suggests Algonkian origin. However, the tribal diversity in the Ohio country and elsewhere in the old northwest with mixed villages (e.g., Delaware and Mingo) militates against precise tribal attributions.

## DECORATIVE ART

Symbols relating to Iroquois cosmology are prevalent in Iroquois old decorative art, usually in porcupine quillwork or, later, beadwork to embellish high status and ceremonial clothing. The stiffness of quills made them suitable for geometric designs in woven, plaited or applique techniques. Designs in quills and, later, seed beads included the "Sky Dome," a half circle resting on two parallel lines with a pair of simplified plant elements springing from the top of the dome. Apparently the dome represents the arc of the sky and the parallel lines the earth. Some plant forms represent the celestial tree of life that stands in the center of the world bearing the sun and moon above its branches. The dome symbol was also often enhanced by elaborate scrollwork and double curves which appeared executed in fine beadwork on women's broadcloth leggings and skirts of the early 19th century. Other motifs included the stylized sun and mythological turtle and other clan symbols. A number of black-dyed buckskin pouches and bags have survived and are held in major museums in North America and Europe. Often they have zigzag and triangular patterns in woven or plaited quillwork in bands, usually of yellow-orange, blue or black, and red colors. Zoomorphic and anthropomorphic designs were also important. The Iroquois also used moosehair to embellish the surface of burden straps and prisoner ties.

During the 16th and early 17th centuries the Iroquois also decorated their pottery and wood carvings with geometric designs. The bowls on their clay pipes were modeled with realistic human and animal forms. The abundant plantlife in the Iroquois homeland suggests the aboriginal use of leaf-like patterns, but there is no certainty that realistic floral patterns pre-date European influence. Nevertheless, the Iroquois pine tree is a core emblem of the Confederacy. It bore luminous blossoms to provide light and its great white roots penetrate the primal turtle in whose back the earth rested. Some scroll and tendril designs were called violets (bowing the head) or fernheads suggesting floral symbolism was indigenous. Some scrolls also represented horns, emblems of chieftainship and high rank.

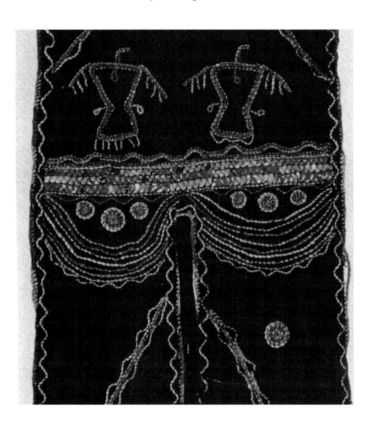

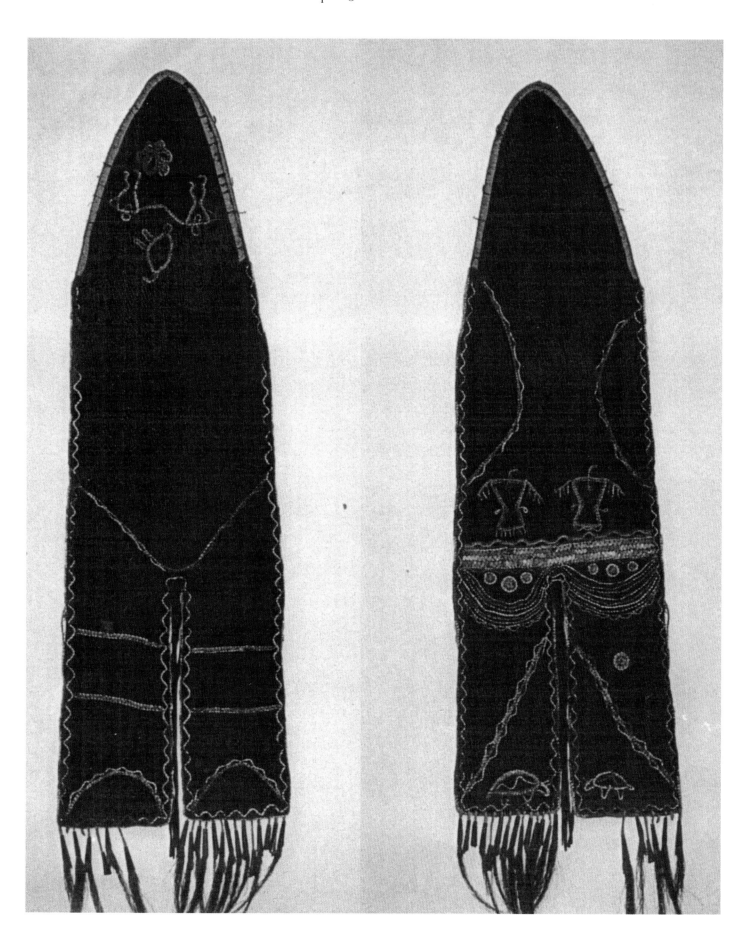

## IROQUOIS BEADED "A" DESIGNS

Used for simple borders — on leggings of both sexes, female skirts and male breechclouts, and moccasin cuffs.

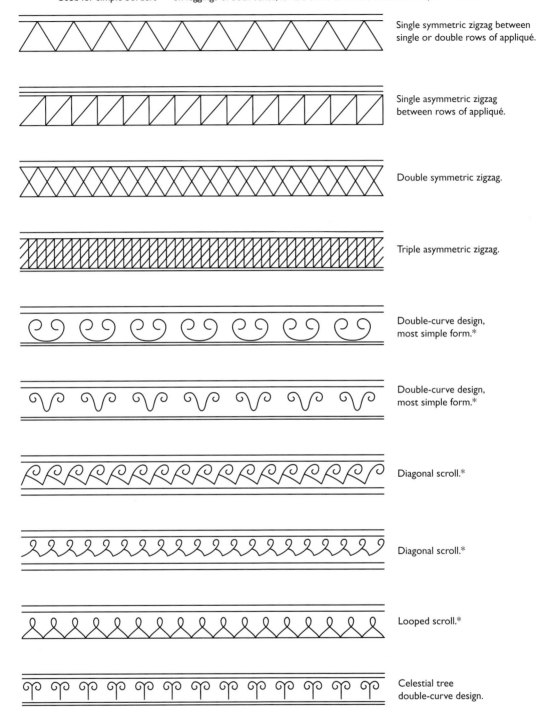

Single symmetric zigzag between single or double rows of appliqué.

Single asymmetric zigzag between rows of appliqué.

Double symmetric zigzag.

Triple asymmetric zigzag.

Double-curve design, most simple form.*

Double-curve design, most simple form.*

Diagonal scroll.*

Diagonal scroll.*

Looped scroll.*

Celestial tree double-curve design.

Any "A" design may be used as the only decorative element on any border inside the ribbon binding. Any single or double line of appliqué may be further ornamented with

* any of these designs may be reversed or inverted.

Double-curve.

Double-curve on
1 row of appliqué,
3 bead rows of lazy-stitch,
row of appliqué.

Grecian scroll.

Entwined double curve.

## DOUBLE-CURVE DESIGNS

Celestial tree.

**Below and Below left:**
Iroquois moccasins, c. 1850,
of commercial leather, velvet,
and beadwork. They were
probably made for sale to
whites.

**Right:** Woman's skirt with beadwork, a drawing of an item collected by Lewis Henry Morgan and presented to the University of the State of New York, Albany, 1851, but the collection was largely destroyed by fire in 1911.

**Opposite and Below:** Recently made but traditional women's cloth skirts decorated with beadwork in early 19th-century style — Schoharie Museum, NY (opposite) and Iroquois Museum, Howes Cave, NY (below).

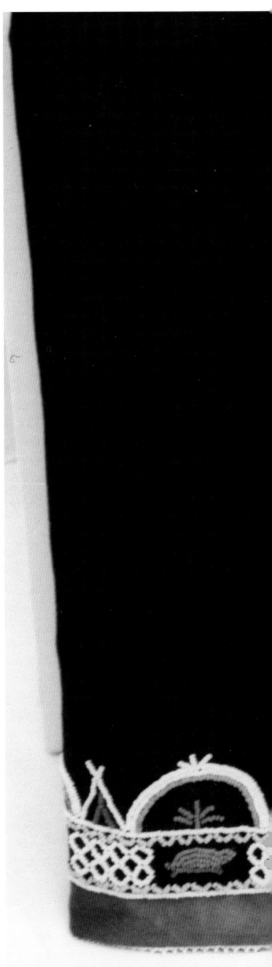

## IROQUOIS BEADED "B" DESIGNS

"B" designs are almost always used to finish off an "A" design. Unlike "A" designs they are never used alone.
The most common "B" design is the "sky dome," and combinations and variations thereof.
The sky dome may be ornamented in many different ways. Like "A" designs "B" designs almost always sit on a foundation of appliqué.

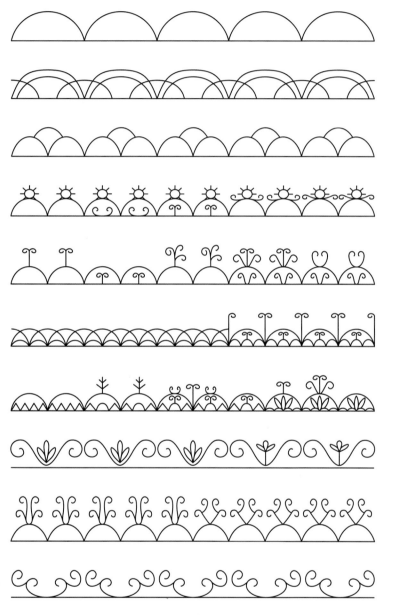

Most simple sky dome.

Intersecting sky domes.

3 domes.

Sky domes with sun and
double-curve ornament.
Four variations.

Domes with celestial tree forms.

**Opposite:** Iroquois pouch of the first half of the 19th century. It is made from red cloth decorated with older, early 19th-century beaded designs.

Combining designs: very often, on older and more elaborate pieces many designs are combined.
Usually, these combined designs consist of one or more "A" designs topped off with a "B" design:

Satin binding.

Edge beading, 2 or 3 beads.

114

Iroquois-type beaded bag — glass beads, black wool broadcloth, silk-ribbon edge-binding, and extended silk top. It measures 7.25 inches (18.4 cm) high by 8 inches (20.3 cm) wide; c. 1830. The intriguing feature on this piece is the use of traditional designs on one side — such as the diamond, stylized heart, and scroll or spiral — and floral motifs on the other. It might be a transitional bag from a traditional artist who was experimenting with floral designs.

## IROQUOIS BEADWORK OF THE 19th CENTURY

The availability of glass beads and trade cloth allowed the Iroquois to create new decorative art forms on clothes and also to produce objects for sale. This played a crucial role in the subsistence of many families on several reservations in New York and Canada. Given a strong sense of design, they began to use glass beads in a wide range of colors on delicately made hats, purses, and other objects — not made for their own use by and large, but to sell to white visitors at such places as Niagara Falls, Saratoga Springs, and Lake George. Changing styles in women's clothes gave rise to the use of hand bags as a fashion accessory. Pouches and bags — garnished at first in small seed beads in designs of lost and now half-forgotten symbols and motifs — found a ready market among the ladies of the time. By the mid-19th century the New York and Canadian Iroquois had developed a style of floral beadwork on objects which they made primarily to satisfy prevailing tastes of the period, with designs using successively larger beads. The designs they used suggest the Iroquois were copying Victorian forms to improve the saleability of their products rather than turning to indigenous designs or the designs fostered by the Ursulines two centuries before. (Nuns of the Ursuline religious order came to Canada in 1639 when Marie de l'Incarnation established a convent. She learned the local languages, including Iroquois, producing Algonkian and Iroquois dictionaries, and successfully taught Indian girls.) This view is supported by the nature of the tourist-oriented objects such as small purses or pouches, and later pincushions, caps, and picture frames. So a flourishing cottage industry was born using a new style of bead embroidery more reflective of European and North American tastes. The beading created an embossed, bas-relief effect with a wide color range. Besides the volume of moccasins, pouches, and pincushions, a popular hat made by the Iroquois was the Glengarry, the Scottish headgear creased lengthwise across the top and trimmed with ribbons at the back. These heavily beaded versions were probably derived from the military uniforms worn by some British regiments serving in Canada (see examples on pages 120–121).

The Tuscarora — geographically close to Niagara — and the Mohawk of Caughnawaga (Kahnawake), close to Montreal, were no doubt the major producers of this material; however, the Allegany Seneca also produced it as one relatively early reference to this type of handicraft is in a memorandum written by a "progressive" Allegany Seneca, Maris Bryant Pierce, dated March 10, 1840. In it Pierce mentions wampum, moccasins, wallets, and work-bags he displayed at a lecture concerning the Six Nations which he gave to whites at Parsipanny, New Jersey. Indian people from several of the above reservation groups seem to have distributed their wares sometimes via middlemen, to locations where white "tourists" would be tempted to purchase their work — one such example being Tugby & Walker's store at Niagara Falls (see page 119).

The beading on two types of work uses the so-called embossed or raised technique, obtained by threading on more beads than required to span the design element so that when stitched the beads arch in a similar manner to Plains Indian "lazy" stitching. Often the beadwork follows a paper pattern or template sewn before the beads are fixed to the surface of the purse or pouch. This also serves as a stiff base on which to bead more easily. The finer of the two styles utilizes fairly heavy multicolored designs but usually incorporates

**Left:** Iroquois-type beaded bag — glass beads, black wool broadcloth, silk-ribbon edge-binding, and silk inlays. It measures 7.25 inches high by 8 inches wide (18.4 cm x 20.3 cm) and dates to 1825–1830. The central design on this large bag has two pairs of outward turning double curves surmounted by a sun symbol. It could be a representation of the celestial sun from the Iroquois creation story.

**Below left:** Iroquois-type beaded bag with a central heart motif — glass beads, red wool broadcloth, cotton lining, and silk-ribbon edge-binding. It measures 6.3 inches high by 6.3 inches wide (16 cm x 16 cm) and dates from the first quarter of the 19th century.

**Above:** Two beaded Iroquois-type card cases (wallets) with bird motifs — glass beads, dark brown velvet, and glazed cotton lining. Each is approximately 4.25 inches wide by 8 inches long (10.7 cm x 20.3 cm) when opened. They date to the mid-19th century.

**Right:** A group of Iroquois beaded cloth purses with traditional geometric and double-curve motif designs; c. 1830–1840 period.

century and through to the early decades of the 20th century inspiring a new range of objects which became popular with souvenir hunters and usually called "whimsies." These objects are usually beaded with larger beads in raised flowers, birds, words, and dates. They come in many shapes, including bags, pincushions, wall hangings, boots, shoes, and matchbox holders. Many such objects are attributed to the Mohawk of Kahnawake, although examples of this form of tourist ornament were sold throughout Iroquoia. Characteristic of these later objects are the long beaded loops hanging along the bottom edges. Specialist beadworkers continue these arts today.

Indian purses were usually constructed on a background of wool flannel, red or blue, sometimes velvet of purple, blue, black, or even green color, backed by a loosely woven cotton cambric or taffeta. The edges are finished with a cotton or silk tape. Some of the older purses have beaded designs that clearly incorporate early Indian design motifs which allow us to make tentative tribal and date attributions.

The earliest known bags and pouches created by the Iroquois were made of buckskin and decorated with porcupine quills. The next generation — made of broadcloth and beadwork — retained old designs such as sun and star motifs, hearts, equal-armed cross, organic, and double-curve motifs. Many early specimens are beaded generally with designs created in very small beads in zigzag patterns, but by the 1840s beadwork was becoming more floralistic. Similar but usually distinctive material was also made by the Micmac (Mi'kmaq) of eastern Canada and the various Abenaki groups of Maine and Quebec.

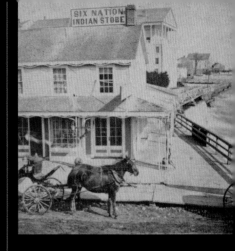

**Above:** 1860s view of Tugby & Walker's Niagara Falls variety store, where Iroquois souvenirs could be purchased. The opening of the Erie Canal in 1825 brought hordes of tourists to the Falls, and by the 1840s Indian fancy beadwork was an important product. Theodore Hulett and his brother opened The Old Curiosity Shop and the Indian Shop to take advantage of this trade. In their 1943 guidebook to the Falls they included the tribes whose work was on sale in their shops: the Tuscarora; Seneca from the Tonawanda Reservation; Allegany Senecas from the Salamanca area; the Cattaraugus Seneca from present-day Irving, NY; and Mohawks from the Montreal area.

**Left:** Six-paneled cap decorated with embossed Iroquois beadwork, c. 1860.

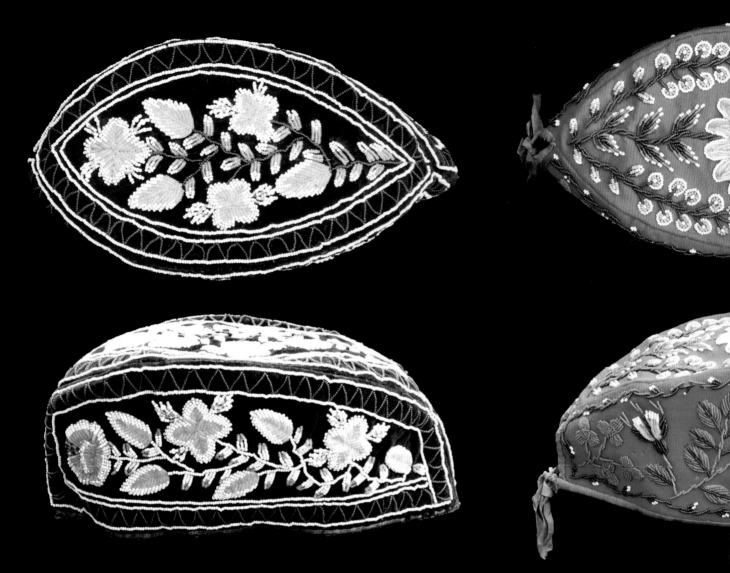

**Above:** Beaded Glengarry cap, possibly Iroquois. Glass beads, navy blue velvet, red silk ribbon edge binding, glazed cotton lining. 5.25 inches wide by 10.5 inches long (13.3 cm x 26.6 cm). Date c. 1840s.

**Right:** Glengarry cap with post-1840 floral designs.

**Above far right:** Iroquois-type beaded Glengarry cap with bird motif. Glass beads, black velvet, red cotton hem tape edge binding. 5.8 inches wide by 10.6 inches long (14.7 cm x 26.9 cm). Mid-19th century.

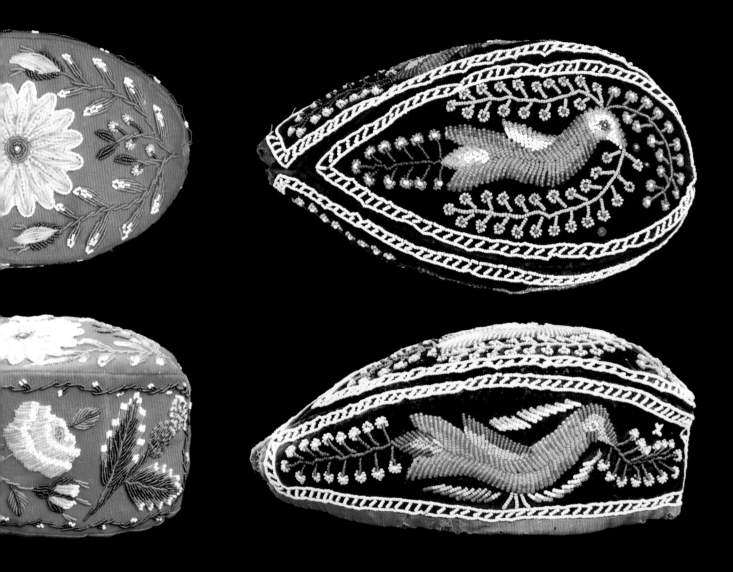

**Above left:** Beaded Glengarry cap, like Seneca. Glass beads, red wool felt, green silk ribbon edge binding, and silk lining. 5.25 inches wide by 9.5 inches long (13.3 cm x 24.1 cm). The large floral motif on the top is stylistically identical to one on a tablecover in the Rochester Museum and Science Center that was made by Caroline Parker. The "art of flowering" that Lewis Henry Morgan attributes to her, where the floral work was depicted in various stages of blossoming, is also evident on this piece.

**Left:** Iroquois beaded Glengarry hats c. 1850.

**Opposite:** Iroquois beaded pouch, first half 19th century. Red cloth with beaded cross and heart designs.

**Far left:** Iroquois purse, c.1820. This red tradecloth pouch is decorated with double-curve and zigzag motifs in very small beads. Some of the design elements are old, traditional, and probably indigenous, indicating an early type of object which became popular later as souvenirs.

**Above and Below:** Two Iroquois cloth flat bags or purses with zigzag beaded designs, c. 1830.

**Left:** Iroquois purse, c. 1830, in dark cloth with zigzag beaded designs.

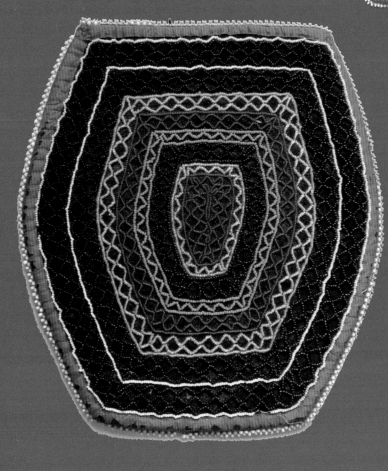

**Opposite:** Beaded pocket book, a drawing after Lewis Henry Morgan, presented to the University of the State of New York, Albany, 1851, a collection largely destroyed by fire in 1911.

**Left and Below left:** Small Iroquois pouch of red trade cloth, silk ribbon border, and beadwork in diamond and "U"-shaped designs typical of the early 19th century. It measures 4 x 4 inches (10.16 cm x 10.16 cm).

**Below:** Tuscarora Indian beadworker Louise Henry working at her home on the Tuscarora Reservation near Niagara Falls, New York State c. 1980. The Tuscarora are one of the six tribes forming the Iroquois Confederacy.

**Right and Far right:** Iroquois purse, probably Mohawk, 6.5 by 6.5 inches (16.5 cm x 16.5 cm). Canadian Museum of Civilization #111-1-1176, collected by James du Pres, Third Earl of Caledon of Tyrone, Captain of the Coldstream Guards.

**Opposite:** One of many shapes of cloth purses made by Iroquois Indians of upper New York state or adjacent Canada for the souvenir markets during the 19th century — this one c. 1860, measuring 5 x 8 inches (12.7 cm x 20.3 cm). The so-called embossed beading is typical of the middle and second half of the century.

**Right:** A larger than usual early 19th century — c. 1830 — pouch constructed of wool cloth and fabric edged with silk. The beadwork is typical Iroquois-type with traditional zigzag and sky-dome designs and embossed leaf-like patterns that gradually succeeded them. A very similar pouch is in the Canadian Museum of Civilization, Gatineau, Quebec, #111-1-1176 (see above). This pouch measures 7.5 x 7.5 inches (19 cm x 19 cm).

**Right:** Heart-shaped red cloth purse made by the Iroquois Indians of upper New York state. Early examples of Iroquois beadwork show geometric or symbolic native designs but later Victorian-inspired floral designs became popular. This one dates to c. 1850 and measures 6.5 inches long x 5 inches wide (16.5 cm x 12.7 cm).

**Far right:** Small Iroquois purse, c. 1850 — possibly Tonawanda Seneca. Note the solid borders and star design.

**Below right:** Common form of purse produced for the souvenir trade. Such bags were made of various cloths, often dark in color and beaded with floral motifs in the embossed or raised style. They usually had a cloth or cord strap added. Some of the many shapes may derive from the sporran of British military influence. This one is c. 1880, measuring 6 x 6 inches (15.2 cm x 15.2 cm).

**Above:** Small purse or pouch of red cloth and lined. The beaded border patterns and star and leaf design suggest this purse was made on the Tonawanda Seneca Reservation in western New York State. It dates to c. 1840 and measures 5 x 4 inches (12.7 cm x 10.2 cm).

**Left and Below left:** Both sides of an Iroquois purse or small pouch which represents a distinctive style with scalloped edges with perimeter solid bands of beadwork. This type of purse has been attributed to the Tonawanda band of Seneca and dates to c. 1850.

**Below:** Red cloth Iroquois purse with beaded borders dating to c. 1840.

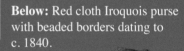

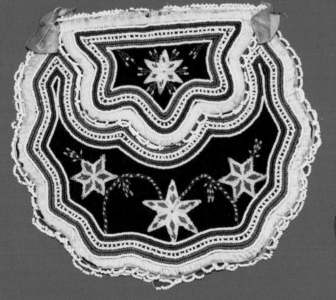

**Above:** A group of beaded Iroquois items including a cap, moccasins, and purses, probably Tuscarora, c. 1860–1880. The objects illustrate the raised or "embossed" beaded technique.

**Opposite, Above and Below right:** A group of Kahnawake (Caughnawaga)-Mohawk souvenir beaded "whimsies" including a valance, hatpin cushions, and boot. c. 1880–1940.

**Right and Center right:** Iroquois "whimsies" — ladies' hatpin cushions with beaded flag and bird motifs, c. 1900. Probably Mohawk, made at Kahnawake (Caughnawaga) near Montreal.

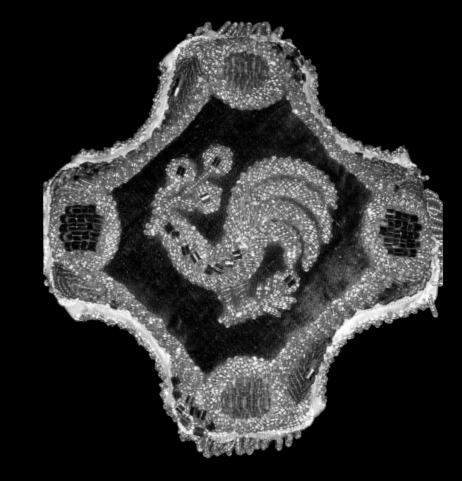

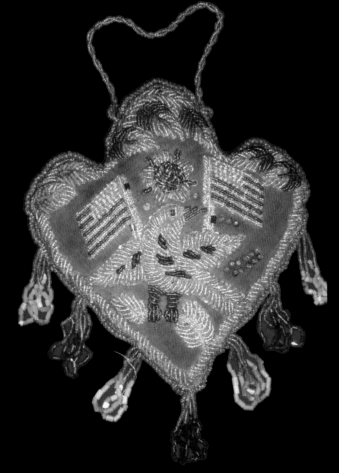

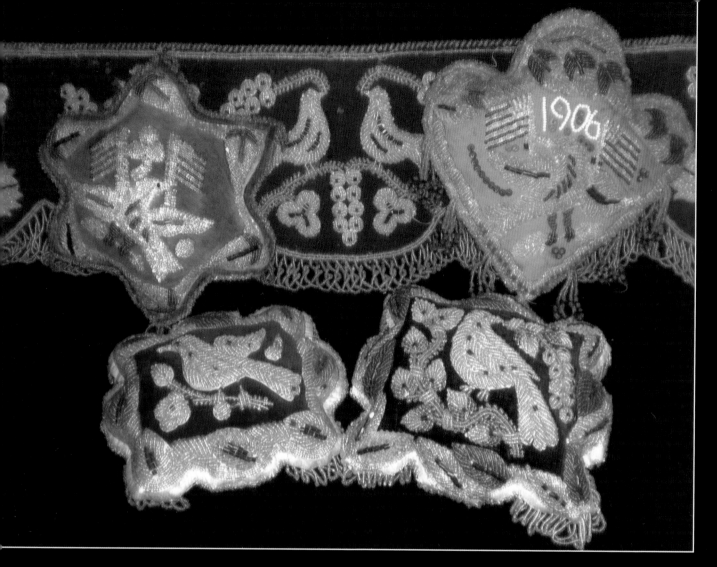

**Above and Right:** A group of 'whimsies' with beaded bird or eagle and US flag designs — hatpin cushions, pillows, and valance. Probably Kahnawake Mohawk, c. 1906.

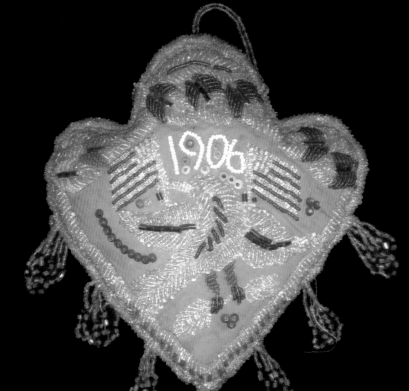

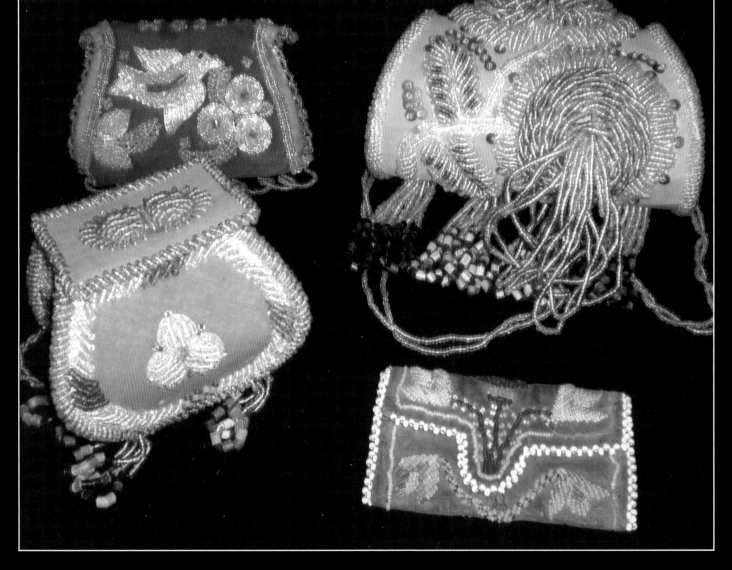

**Above and Left:** Group of Iroquois beaded purse and needle case "whimsies," probably Kahnawake Mohawk, c. 1900–1910.

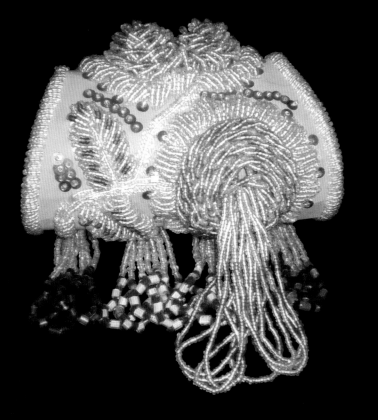

**This spread:** Views of a Mohawk beaded box, c. 1915. Souvenir beadwork purses, boxes, picture frames, etc., were made by the Mohawks of Caughnawaga for sale in nearby Montreal and other tourist locations and were popular in the late 19th and early 20th centuries. This one measures 6 inches high x 7 inches wide (15.2 cm x 17.7 cm) without fringe. A similar example can be found in the National Museum of the American Indian.

**Opposite, Below left:** A c. 1905 six-lobed beaded pincushion of a type made in the late 19th century and early 20th century for the souvenir trade. Often attributed to the Mohawk of Caughnawaga. This one measures 8 inches (20.3 cm) across.

# Chapter 4: People

**Opposite:** Brant as painted by Jan Verelst in 1710. Note bear totem at right.

**Above and Below:** An ad for an 1862 race and "Deerfoot" c. 1890.

**Wallace "Mad Bear" Anderson** (1927–1985) A Tuscarora political activist in the 1950s and 1960s, he was a veteran of Saipan, Okinawa, and Korea. He was a member of a party of Indians who went to Cuba in 1959 and met Fidel Castro. He was involved in the Tuscaroras' resistance to giving up part of their reservation to the New York State Power Authority in the 1950s.

**Lewis Bennett or "Deerfoot"** (c. 1830–1895) A Seneca from Cattaraugus Reservation, he had been a professional runner competing in England in 1861–1862 and won against most English competitors.

**Mary ("Molly") Brant** (c. 1736–1796) The Mohawk half-sister of Joseph Brant and third wife of Sir William Johnson, she learned to read and write English at boarding school in Schenectady. Molly never forgave the Americans for attacking Johnson Hall and its confiscation. After the Revolution the Americans offered her estates back, but she refused them and remained in Canada.

**Brant or Sagayengwarahton ("Old Smoke")** (d. before 1753) He was a Mohawk war chief of the Bear Clan, as confirmed by the totemic animal recorded at the bottom of his portrait painted by Verelst in London in 1710 when a member of a deputation of "American Kings." His grandson is likely the Brant who married Margaret, a Seneca widow already with two children, Mary (Molly) and Joseph, who, taking his stepfather's name, became the famous Joseph Brant. Conversion to the Anglican faith saw many Mohawk adopt English names.

**John Brant or Ahyouwaighs** (1794–1832) A son of Joseph Brant by his third wife Catherine, he was born September 27, 1794. He received a good English education, but also took part in the war against the Americans 1812–1815. John and his sister Elizabeth lived in the family residence at the head of Lake Ontario although their mother returned to Six Nations Reserve after the death of Joseph Brant. In 1821 John visited England on tribal business which was unsuccessful. He died of cholera and is buried alongside his father at the Mohawk Chapel on the edge of the Six Nations Reserve, Ontario. (See image on page 138.)

**Joseph Brant or Thayendanegea** (1742 or 1743–1807) His Indian name refers to

**Top:** John Brant.

**Above:** Joseph Brant, after Catlin and Ames.

**Opposite:** Hendrick painted by Verelst in 1710. Note wolf totem.

**Below:** Cornplanter, after a painting by F. Bartoli, 1796.

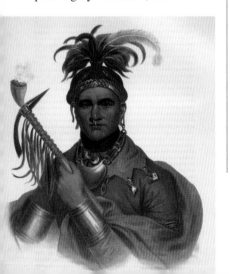

two wagers (sticks as in bets) bound together. His parents were Canajoharie Mohawks but his father was killed in the Ohio country and his mother remarried an Indian known to the whites as Brant. His career as a warrior began at the age of 13 when he joined the Mohawks at the Battle of Lake George in 1755. He and his half-sister Molly became protégés of Sir William Johnson. Joseph was sent to Dr. Wheelock's school in Connecticut, while Molly became Johnson's third wife. He was also present at the Battle at Fort Niagara in 1759 and took part in the Pontiac War of 1763. In November 1775 Brant accompanied Guy Johnson to London, the first of two visits, and King George III conferred upon him the rank of captain. He devoted his energies to the British cause during the Revolution, and was raised by Gov. Carleton to the rank of colonel. He may have been present at Cherry Valley 1778 and is associated by the Americans with atrocities on the frontier. After the British defeat he moved to Canada and was instrumental in obtaining the Grand River tract (Six Nations Reserve) although he lived the remainder of his life as an English squire at Burlington, Ontario, and was criticized for conveyancing land on the Six Nations Reserve to whites. He supervised a new edition of the Prayer Book and Psalms in the Mohawk language and is reported to have translated a version of the Gospel of St. Mark. He is buried in the grounds of the Mohawk Chapel close to the city which bears his name, Brantford.

**Canasatego** (c. 1684–1750) Onondaga chief, and a Confederacy Chief of the Iroquois, he is remembered as acting for Pennsylvania's governor to condemn the Delawares as "women" and to forbid them to sell land thereafter, during the Easton Treaty of 1742. After this the Delawares were ordered to leave the Forks of the Delaware and Minisinks and move to Wyoming (Wilkes-Barre) and Shamokin (Sunbury). He was an Iroquois spokesman again at Lancaster (1744), at Onondaga and Albany (1745), and Philadelphia (1749) with Weiser and Clinton respectively.

**Cornplanter or Gyantwahia** (c. 1740–1836) His name signifies "by what one plants." A Seneca chief on the Allegheny River, western New York, he is also known as John O'Bail after his father, an Albany Dutch trader. He fought for the British during the American Revolution, but later became friendly with the Americans and accepted the white man's lifestyle at his model community in northern Pennsylvania. He participated in the treaties of Ft. Stanwix (1784), Ft. Harmer (1789), and Halftown (1790); also present at Canandaigua (1794) and Big Tree (1797). He received a personal land grant (Cornplanter Reserve) from the governor of Pennsylvania. He was half-brother to Handsome Lake, the religious reformer.

**Farmer's Brother or Honayawas** (c. 1740–1841) A Seneca war chief who fought bravely for the Americans during the War of 1812, he was prominent at the Battle of Chippewa (1814). He was buried with military honors alongside Red Jacket and other Senecas in the Forest Lawn Cemetery in Buffalo, NY. He was befriended by George Washington who was a noted farmer, hence Honayawas' popular name.

**French Margaret** (c. 1700–?) A daughter or relative of Madame Montour, she married Mohawk Chief Peter Quebec and lived in the Ohio country and, after 1745, at Lycoming Creek (Williamsport). About 1756 her family moved north to the Chemung River, NY, at Assinisink (Painted Post) where her son-in-law Eghohowin was chief helping English prisoners during the French and Indian War. She had several children among them probably Queen Esther.

**Above:** Tom Longboat participates in a sports exhibition at Ebbets Field, Brooklyn, NY, on July 26, 1913.

**Below:** E. Pauline Johnson.

**Guyasuta or Kayahsota** (c. 1725–1794) Seneca chief and half king on the Allegheny-Ohio rivers, he accompanied Washington on his failed trip to remove the French in 1753. He was with the French at Ft. Duquesne in 1755 and tried to prevent Pontiac's War of 1763. He finally fought on the British side in the American Revolution but remained in the United States at the close of the war.

**Handsome Lake or Ganiodariyo** (1735–1815) His name is one of the position titles for the men's Grand Council. He was a well-connected Seneca (half-brother of Cornplanter and uncle of Red Jacket) who became a divine following a long illness, after which he claimed to have had a series of visions and messages from the creator. He preached his "Good Word" with practical solutions to the problems of alcohol. Most of his ministry was at Cornplanter's Town, Cold Spring, and Tonawanda, but he died at Onondaga in 1815. His teachings are still recited in modern Longhouses encouraging the continuance of the thanksgiving ceremonies. His grandson, Shosheowa (Jimmy Johnson) was responsible for codifying some of his teachings in 1826 at the request of the faith-keepers at Tonawanda.

**Hendrick or Teyonhehkwen** (c. 1660–1735) Also known as Henry Peters or Dutch Henry, he was a Mohawk from Fort Hunter, Montogomery County, NY and converted to the Protestant faith about 1690. He was already a chief by the time of the treaties at Montreal and Albany in 1701. In 1710 he — along with three other American "Kings" — was part of a deputation to London and presented at the court of Queen Anne. He was painted by Jan Verelst in one of the four full-length portraits which includes a reference to his Wolf Clan affiliation (see page 139). He was a supporter of the Covenant Chain, a network of friendship between the British and Indian nations.

**Hendrick or Thoyanoguen** (1692–1755) Also known as Hendrick Peters or King Hendrick, he was a Mohawk leader and member of the Bear Clan from Canajoharie or Upper Mohawk Castle. Until recently he was confused and combined as one with Teyonhehkwen, also known as Hendrick. He was born in Westfield, MA to a Mahican father and Mohawk woman. He is said to have visited London in 1740 and was painted in a gold-fringed coat and tri-corn hat (see engraving after the painting on page 25), although the visit has not been verified, and the painting may have been done in America. The league's council at Onondaga gave him authority to speak on behalf of the Six Nations and some of his speeches were highly critical of British policies. A firm friend of Sir William Johnson, Hendrick was killed fighting with him at Lake George in September 1755. A life-size statue of them is in Lake George Park, NY (see page 30).

**John of Canajoharie or Ho Nee Yeath Taw No Row (probably Honientanoron, "Fine Shanks")** (Dates unknown.) A Mohawk Chief and one of the Four Kings at the court of Queen Anne. Brother of Hendrick (perhaps only in an Indian sense) and both Warrior Chiefs at that time. Hendrick was raised to a Confederacy Chief later, but nothing more is heard of John after their return to America. (See photo on page 26.)

**E. (Emily) Pauline Johnson or Tekahionwake ("Double Life")** (1861–1913) A daughter of a mixed-blood Mohawk sachem, George Martin Johnson, and an English woman from Bristol, she was born at Chiefswood, a large house on the edge of the Six Nations Reserve near Brantford. It was here Queen Victoria's son Prince Arthur, Duke of Connaught was adopted as honorary Chief in 1869. Pauline Johnson became one of Canada's foremost poetesses and made two tours of England. She died in Vancouver.

**Kateri Tekakwitha** (1656–1680) The "Lily of the Mohawks" was a Mohawk/Algonkian, her mother being a captive Christian, born at Ossernenon, a Mohawk village. She moved to the Catholic missions near Montreal where she died aged 24. However, legend has it that on death her face, disfigured by smallpox, apparently cleared. Her remains are at the Church of St. Francis Xavier au Sault at the Indian village of Caughnawaga, and she was beatified in 1980. She was cannonized on October 21, 2012.

**Logan, or John Shickellamy or Tachnechdorus** (?–c. 1786) Son of Shickellamy, Logan succeeded his father as half king at Shamokin in 1749, and helped Pennsylvania make the Albany Purchase of 1754. Some of his people were killed by the Paxton Boys at Conestoga in 1763. About 1770 he joined the Mingos in the Ohio country where Heckewelder met him and where 13 members of his family were murdered in 1774, following which he joined the Shawnee fighting the Virginians in the so-called Lord Dunmore's War. He was assassinated by a nephew. A monument stands to him at Auburn, New York.

**Tom Longboat** (1886–1949) An Onondaga from Six Nations Reserve, Ontario, Longboat was the leading Canadian athlete of his generation. Marathon runner, winner of the Boston Marathon in a record time, unfortunately he collapsed from sunstroke in the 1908 London Olympics. He turned professional and continued to win races, although wounded in World War I. He is buried behind the Onondaga Longhouse at Six Nations.

**Madame Montour** (c. 1684–c. 1752) Reputed to have been a daughter of a governor of Canada and taken prisoner by the Iroquois when about 10 years old, her first husband is said to have been Roland Montour, a Seneca. Later she married Big Tree, an Oneida who took the name Hunter in compliment to a governor of New York. She was interpreter at a conference at Albany in 1711 and at Philadelphia in 1727. After 1727 she lived at a village on the west branch of the Susquehanna, at present-day Montourville, and later in the Allegheny-Ohio country.

**Dr. Oronhyateka or Peter Martin** (1841–1907) Six Nations Iroquois, whose name means "Burning Cloud." He married Irene Hill, great granddaughter of Chief Joseph Brant. Peter Martin was an official interpreter for the chiefs during a visit of the Prince of Wales to Six Nations. The prince encouraged him to go to Oxford University, England. Queen Victoria sent him a reproduction throne (now in the Royal Ontario Museum, Toronto) on his return to Canada. In 1871, be became a member of Canada's National Rifle Team and in 1878 he was, remarkably, accepted into the Independent Order of Foresters (hitherto open only to "white males") and promoted the organization heavily during his life.

**Ely Samuel Parker** (1828–1895) A Seneca from Tonawanda Reservation, of mixed blood but a grandson of Red Jacket, he was well-educated, and he and his family collaborated with Lewis Henry Morgan for an epic work on the Iroquois, *The League of the Ho-de-no-sau-nee or Iroquois*, first published in 1851, the same year he was named one of the 50 sachems of the Haudenosaunee, succeeding former Chief John Blacksmith. The dedication to Morgan's book reads: "To Ha-sa-no-an-da, (Ely S. Parker), a Seneca Indian, this work, the materials of which are the fruit of our joint researches, is inscribed: 'In acknowledgement of the obligations, and in testimony of the friendship of the author.' " Parker studied law and engineering but when the American Civil War broke out he joined the Union Army. He became Gen. Ulysses S. Grant's military secretary and

**Above:** The first Canadian rifle team to represent Canada against England includes Dr. Oronhyateka (third from right in foreground).

**Below:** Lt.-Col. Ely Parker at Grant's headquarters in 1865.

**Right:** Washington and Gist visit Indian Queen Alliquippa in December 1753. An ally of the British forces, Washington gave her a gift, "I made her a present of a match-coat and a bottle of rum, which latter was thought much the better present of the two."

**Opposite, top:** Clinton Rickard — he holds a wampum belt which symbolizes the Iroquois refusal of Christianity, the cross being set apart from three human figures.

**Opposite, center:** While Clinton Rickard was a veteran of the Spanish-American War, his son, Clark, was a veteran of World War II. In this phototgraph of them, c. 1948, Clinton wears a moose-skin shirt with beaded designs representing hands holding the Covenant Chain symbol of peace. Grouped around the American eagle are 13 stars for the original states and six other stars symbolizing the Iroquois nations.

**Opposite, bottom:** Eleazar Williams.

**Below:** Red Jacket, after a painting by Charles Bird King in 1828. He is wearing the original silver medal presented to him by George Washington, which was decorated: on recto, Red Jacket smoking a long pipe, George Washington on left with right hand extended, below the inscription: "George Washington / President / 1792"; on verso, there is the presidential seal.

wrote the document of surrender signed by Robert E. Lee at Appomattox Court House. He rose to the rank of brigadier-general.

**Queen Alliquippa** (1690–1754) A Seneca and acknowledged chief of an Indian village in the vicinity of the Forks of the Ohio, she is said to have met William Penn at New Castle, Delaware in 1701. Later her home was western Pennsylvania where Conrad Weiser visited her in 1748 and George Washington in 1753. She died at Aughwick, PA where she had settled with other friendly Indians after Washington's surrender at Fort Necessity at the start of the French and Indian War. Her son, Cassiowea, known as Newcastle, a war chief, negotiated with hostile Delawares and Shawnees during their conflict but died of smallpox in 1756.

**Queen Esther** (c. 1720–1790) Probably a daughter of French Margaret, Esther married Eghohowin, a Munsee chief, and subsequently lived on the north branch of the Susquehanna River near the Moravian mission (Ulster). After her husband's death in 1772 her village (Queen Esther's Town) lay between present-day West Athens and Milan (Tioga Point). She protected settlers at the beginning of the Revolution but possibily killed prisoners after the battle of Wyoming — thus inspiring stories of the masaacre. After the war she is said to have remarried a Tuscarora and moved north to Cayuga Lake. Esther's sister was Catherine Montour, whose village was at Seneca Lake, NY (Shequaga), and her son Roland Montour joined Col. John Butler's Rangers during the Revolutionary War. The Montour descendants are at Six Nations Reserve, Ontario.

**Red Jacket** (c. 1756–1830) A Seneca chief born probably at Canoga, NY, during the American Revolution, he and his tribe espoused the British cause. His distinctive dress, wearing brilliant red jackets provided by British officers, gave rise to his popular name. However, he refused to stand and fight the Americans at Canandaiga during the invasion of Seneca country by Gen. Sullivan in 1779 and was accused of cowardice. Later he championed the customs, religion, and institutions of his tribesmen and strove manfully to prevent the sale of lands, opposing schools and Christianity, but his wife's conversion forced him to acquiesce. In 1792 he, with a delegation of Iroquois chiefs, visited Philadelphia when Washington gave him the Peace Medal shown in his portrait. He signed the treaties with the Americans at Canandaigua (1794) and Big Tree (1797). and died in 1830 within the limits of the old Buffalo Creek Reservation near Buffalo, NY.

**Clinton Rickard** (1882–1971) Tuscarora founding member of the Indian Defence League of America in 1926, he worked tirelessly for the rights of Iroquois people and was invited to attend the League of Nations to seek justice for the Six Nations. He was a veteran of the Spanish-American War in the Philippines. He was prominent in the re-establishment of the right of Iroquois to pass freely without taxation between the US and Canada, as provided by the Jay Treaty of 1794 between the US and Great Britain.

**Shickellamy or Swatana (Swataney)** (?–1748) A Cayuga warrior chief whose father was French and mother Cayuga (or perhaps full French), he was captured by Indians and adopted by Oneidas. He was sent by the Iroquois to the Forks of the Susquehanna River (Shamokin) as half king. He married a Cayuga woman of the Wolf Clan so his four sons were all Cayugas in the Iroquois fashion. They were: Arahpot (unhappy Jake, killed by Catawbas in 1744); Tachnechdorus (John Shickellamy or Logan); Tahgahjute (James Logan or Lame James); and John Petty or Petit . For several years he was Pennsyvania's principal channel of negotiations with the Iroquois and collaborated closely with James Logan and Conrad Weiser.

**Scarouyady** (?–1757 or 1758) A famous Oneida warrior chief who on the death of Tanacharison became half king for the combined Mingo, Delaware, and Shawnee. Conrad Weiser met him in 1748 at Logstown. He was with Washington and Gen. Braddock in their attempts to remove the French in the west, at Ft. Necessity (1754) and Monongahela (1755) respectively.

**Tanaghrisson or Tanacharison** (1700–1754) A Seneca Chief, but perhaps a Catawba by birth and captured by the Seneca, he was sent by the Iroquois in 1747 as half king to the Ohio Indians, especially to the Delawares, while Scarouyady was given authority over the Shawnees. Recognized spokesman for all the British-allied Ohio Indians, both conferred with Conrad Weiser at Logstown in 1748. He protested to the French after they built forts in the region calling for their removal, which failed. He joined with George Washington in failed attempts to remove the French military forces from the area in 1754 and died in October of that year.

**Eleazar Williams** (1787–1858) Born and raised among the Mohawks, he attended a missionary school at Longmeadow, MA and became a Protestant missionary to the Oneida. He helped them and other nations who were being pushed off their lands by speculators, and in 1820 led a delegation to Wisconsin to negotiate with the Menomini and Winnebago for territory around Green Bay. From 1839 onward he started to claim that he was the lost French Dauphin, the child of Louis XVI and Marie Antoinette who had been spirited away to America for safe-keeping when his parents were deposed and killed during the French Revolution, but this claim was effectively refuted by Henry de Courcy, the New York correspondent for *L'Univers* of Paris.

**Above:** Sir Edmund Andros (1637 –1714), Governor General of New England, c.1690.

**Below:** Sir William Johnson, engraved by Charles Spooner, after a painting by T. Adams, published 1756. He was named Warragh-i-yagey ("doer of great things" or "chief big business") by the Six Nations and in 1760 was given the title of sachem. Guy Johnson — William's nephew and son-in-law — succeeded his uncle as Indian Superintendent until 1782 when he was succeeded by William's son by Catherine Weisenberg, John Johnson.

## IMPORTANT NON-INDIANS IN IROQUOIS (SIX NATIONS) HISTORY

**Sir Edmund Andros** (1637–1714) Architect of the 17th-century Covenant Chain, which was an alliance of Indian tribes — under the general leadership of the Iroquois — and the English colonies under the supervision of New York: a partnership aimed mainly at French trading alliances. He signed a major treaty with the Iroquois at Albany in 1677.

**Henry Bouquet** (1719–1765) A Swiss mercenary, an officer in the British forces, active in the Ohio region during Pontiac's War (1763–1765), he was involved in negotiations for the release of white captives from the Delawares and Shawnees.

**John Butler** (1728–1796) New York Loyalist, friend of the Iroquois, he raised Butler's Rangers and raided the Wyoming Valley in 1778. Commissioned colonel, he was defeated by Sullivan at Newtown in 1779. His son, Walter, led the Cherry Valley raid.

**Louis-Hector de Calliere** (1648–1703) Successor to Frontenac as governor of New France, he negotiated the treaty of 1701 with the Iroquois and others.

**Samuel de Champlain** (c. 1570–1635) Founder of Quebec. He organized expeditions to Huronia and against the Iroquois 1609–1615, which led to Mohawk–French hostility.

**Daniel Claus** (1727–1787) German involved with British Indian affairs, first with Conrad Weiser in 1750 and later with refugee Mohawks in Canada. His son William was also involved with Indian Affairs in Ontario (Upper Canada).

**George Croghan** (1718–1782) Indian trader and land speculator, he was Sir William Johnson's deputy agent in 1756. He traveled constantly to negotiate with tribes for the British cause.

**Marquis de Denonville** (1637–1710) Governor of New France 1685–1689, he invaded Seneca country in 1687. The Iroquois retaliated at La Chine in 1689.

**Simon Girty** (1741–1818) Captured by the Seneca in 1756, he played a prominent part in savage warfare with Americans in the Ohio River region 1778–1794. A fur trader and supporter of the British, he was hated by the Americans during and after the Revolution.

**Sir Frederick Haldimand** (1718–1791) Swiss-born officer in the British forces, he was appointed Governor General of Quebec in 1777. He provided lands for refugee Iroquois in Canada after the American Revolution.

**Sir William Johnson** (1715–1774) Anglo-Irish merchant and land speculator, he came to America in 1738. He had a strong association with the Mohawks and rose to great power after being commissioned Superintendent of Indian Affairs at the onset of the French and Indian War. Created baronet after his victory over the French at Lake George in 1755, his third wife was Molly Brant, half-sister of Joseph Brant.

**Samuel Kirkland** (1741–1808) Protestant missionary to the Oneidas, his influence probably kept the Iroquois from participating in Lord Dunmore's War between the Shawnees and Virginia, and later kept the Oneidas attached to the Americans during the Revolution.

**Rene-Robert de La Salle** (1643–1687) Trader and explorer of the Great Lakes and Mississippi.

**James Logan** (1674–1751) Pennsylvanian Quaker merchant and official, he was heavily involved in Indian affairs with Conrad Weiser and Shickellamy.

**Alexander McKee** (1735–1799) Indian agent and fur trader associated with George Croghan, he married into the Shawnee, organized Indian resistance against the Americans in the Ohio country, and later moved to Canada.

**Major John Norton or Teyoninhokarawen (Te yo in ho kalawen)** (c. 1760–1826 or 1831) Son of a Scottish mother, his father was claimed to be a Cherokee captured as a boy by the British at the town of Keowee, who later came to Britain. Born and educated in Scotland, Norton joined the British army in Ireland and then in North America. He was in Ohio Country and at Tippecanoe in 1791, but in Upper Canada by 1794 working as a teacher and interpreter in several Iroquois communities including the Six Nations. He became a protégé of Joseph Brant and appointed a Pine Tree Chief. In later life he traveled in Cherokee country, Arkansas territory, and Mexico. Some historians believe he was wholly Scottish with no native American antecedents.

**Pierre Radisson** (c. 1640–1710) Explorer of the Great Lakes, he was taken captive by the Iroquois but escaped via the Dutch at Ft. Orange. He accompanied the French Jesuits to Onondaga in 1657, but later turned against France and joined the English, co-foundeding the Hudson's Bay Company with Groseilliers in 1670.

**John Graves Simcoe** (1752–1806) First British governor of Upper Canada 1791–1796, he negotiated with the Iroquois concerning land grants and cessions. His memorial is in Exeter Cathedral, England.

**John Sullivan** (1740–1795) A major-general, he led one of the two invasions of Iroquoia in 1779, destroying crops and forty Indian villages. (The other was led by Maj.-Gen. James Clinton).

**Alexandre de Tracy** (1596–1670) General of the French army in North America that invaded Mohawk country destroying villages and crops in 1666.

**George Washington** (1732–1799) Surveyor, land speculator, soldier, and finally president of the new United States, Washington was commissioned by Virginia in 1753 and sent to warn the French out of the Ohio country. The French rejected his efforts and Washington returned with troops and attacked a French party. He surrendered to the French in 1754 and later served under Braddock and Forbes in campaigns against Fort Duquesne in the French and Indian War. His later history is well covered!

**Conrad Weiser** (1696–1760) A Palatine German, interpreter, soldier, and Pennsylvania official, he was an important link man between the Six Nations and the colonial government together with James Logan and Shickellamy.

**Asher Wright** (1803–1875) Protestant missionary to the Senecas at Buffalo Creek and later Cattaraugus, he protested fraudulent treaties and secured consessions.

**Above:** Maj. John Norton after a painting by Mary Ann Knight, an accomplished English miniaturist. Norton became a protégé of Joseph Brant and appointed a Pine Tree Chief according to Iroquois custom. He represented the Six Nations in England in 1804 and is noted for translating the Gospel of St. John into the Mohawk language in 1805. At the outbreak of the War of 1812 he joined Gen. Brock at Detroit and was active in the Niagara area during the war. He was present at the battles at Queenston and Chippawa, leading Iroquois warriors. He again visited England in 1815 with his second wife and son, but was less successful in his diplomatic discourse.

**Below:** A 1781 engraving of George Washington by John Norman, who is believed to be the first engraver in America to produce a portrait of Washington.

# Chapter 5: Gazetteer

**Akwesasne** ("where the grouse drums") A Mohawk settlement in northern New York, originally an offshoot from Caughnawaga, founded 1754. Mainly Catholic, the 33 sq. mile modern reserve — the Mohawk Nation at Akwesasne — spans between the US and Canada; also called St. Regis after the river that flows into the St. Lawrence at the village of St. Regis.

**Allegany** Seneca reservation of c. 44 sq. mile area near Salamanca, NY.

**Aughwick** Indian village, pro-British during French and Indian War, just north of modern Shirleysburgh, PA.

**Bay of Quinte** or **Tyendinaga** A Mohawk reserve, of 27.5 sq. mile area, near Deseronto, Ontario, founded in 1784 by Mohawk followers of John Deseronto and the Hill brothers (Aaron and Isaac) after leaving Lachine.

**Big Tree** A Seneca village on the Genesee River near Genesco, NY.

**Brotherton** or **Brothertown** Mixed New England Algonkians settled on land provided by the Oneida near Oriskany, NY, in 1774, and named the settlement Brotherton. They moved to Wisconsin in the 19th century.

**Buffalo Creek** Iroquois villages in western New York established in 1780 after the devastating Sullivan Expedition. It became a reservation but was subsequently sold

Chiefswood, home and birth place of Emily Pauline Johnson, Mohawk poetess and theatrical performer, daughter of Chief George Johnson and his English wife Emily Howells. Recently restored and opened as a museum, this is a 2004 photo.

Anglican Christ Church on the Tyendinaga Reserve. Note the flags, Mohawk, Canadian, and Union in front of the memorial to men of the reserve who gave their lives in World War II.

with most of western New York in dubious sales to the Ogden Land Company. Asher Wright and the Quakers were instrumental in helping the Iroquois regain Allegany and Cattaraugus reservations.

**Canajoharie** A Mohawk village near present-day Canajoharie, NY.
**Canandaigua** A Seneca village near present-day Canandaigua, NY.
**Catherine's Town** Home of Catherine Montour 1758–1779, Seneca Lake, NY.
**Cattaraugus** ("stinking banks") Seneca reservation, of about 33.5 sq. miles area, in western NY.
**Caughnawaga** ("at the rapids") (1) Mohawk village near Auriesville, NY (also known as Ossernenon), today the only excavated Iroquois village in the US.
(2) The village and reserve (Kahnawake), near Montreal where some Mohawks and Oneidas settled in 1676.
**Cayadutta** Early Mohawk village near Sammonsville, NY.
**Cayuga** Main village of the Cayuga, on the eastern shore of Lake Cayuga, Union Springs, NY.
**Chiefswood** Home and birth place of E. Pauline Johnson, Mohawk poetess and theatrical performer, daughter of Chief George Johnson and his English wife Emily Howells. Recently, it was restored and opened as a museum
**Chillicothe** Name of several Shawnee villages in Ohio.
**Christ Church** An Anglican church on the Tyendinaga Reserve, Ontario, that is home

**Above:** Fort Chambly today.

**Below:** Contemporary plan of Fort Frontenac.

**Right:** The ruins of Fort Frederic, Crown Point, NY, c. 1902.

to descendants of the Fort Hunter Mohawks from the Mohawk Valley in New York. They had operated from Lachine during the American Revolution. This church shares with the Mohawk Chapel (St. Paul's) at Six Nations the communion silver given to the Iroquois chiefs by Queen Anne during their visit to London in 1710.

**Chugnut** Indian village, mixed Delaware, Shawnees, Conoys, Nanticokes, Mahicans etc., near Binghamton, NY.

**Fort Chambly** French fort built in 1686 at Chambly, Quebec. Captured by the Americans during the Revolution, it was destroyed on their retreat. It was repaired by a private purchaser in the late 19th century and today is a Canadian National Historic Site.

**Fort Crown Point or Fort Frederic** French fort near the southern end of Lake Champlain. Destroyed in 1759, the British built a new fort that was taken by Capt. Seth Warner in 1775, it was abandoned finally in 1780. Today it is a US State Historic Site.

**Fort Le Boeuf** French fort near Waterford, PA. It was burned down during Pontiac's Rebellion but is notable in US history because it was visited by George Washington, who deliverd a message to the French garrison commander in late 1753.

**Fort Erie** Originally a French outpost, the British built a new fort on the Niagara River in 1764. Best-known for the siege of 1814 when it was held by American troops in face of a British attack, it is today a Canadian National Historic Site.

**Fort Hunter** British fort, Schoharie Creek, NY. It was built in 1712 near one of the main Mohawk settlements — named Lower Mohawk Castle by the colonists. Hendrick Peters, one of the four "Kings" who visited Queen Anne in 1710, was a sachem here.

**Fort Frontenac** French fort, Kingston, Ontario. Originally Fort Cataraqui, it was rebuilt by the British in 1783. A Canadian National Historic Site, it is the location of the Canadian Army Command and Staff College.

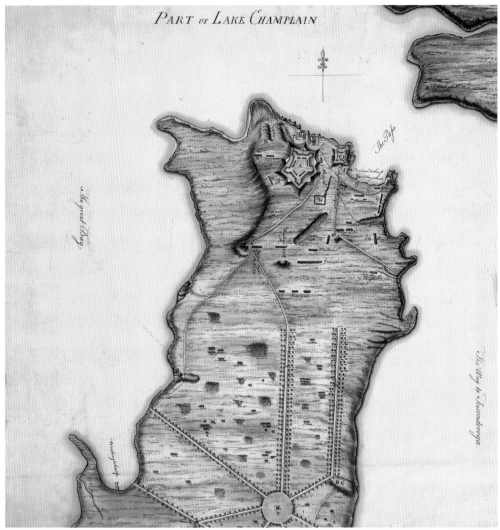

PART OF LAKE CHAMPLAIN

**Left:** Plan of the fort and fortress at Crown Point with their environs and with "the disposition of the English Army under the command of Genl. Amherst encamp'd there 1759."

**Below left:** Fort Niagara, scene of Sir William Johnson's victory over the French in July 1759. He took command of regulars, provincials, and 900 Iroquois warriors, during the French and Indian War.

**Right:** Fort Johnson.

**Below right:** Painting dated 1912 of Fort Orange by Elmer E. Garnsey at Alexander Hamilton US Custom House, New York, NY.

**Below:** Plan of Fort William Henry.

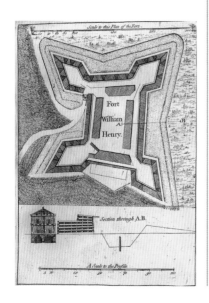

**Fort Johnson** Old Fort Johnson is the original limestone house built by Sir William Johnson, Superintendent of Indian Affairs. The fort was home to William, Catherine Weisenberg, Molly Brant, John Johnson, and family throughout the French and Indian War. Today the fort is a museum.

**Fort Niagara** Scene of Sir William Johnson's victory over the French in July 1759 after he took command of regulars, provincials, and 900 Iroquois warriors during the French and Indian War. It was finally ceded to the United States after the War of 1812 and in continued use until deactivated in 1963. Today it is a state park and museum.

**Fort Orange** Early Dutch fort at Albany, NY. Abandoned by the British after the building of Fort Frederic, itself demolished in 1790.

**Fort Presque Isle** French fort built 1753 at present-day Erie, PA. Rebuilt by the British in 1759, captured in Pontiac's Rebellion, in 1763 the fort was taken by Indians and the garrison killed after it surrendered. The present blockhouse was built in 1880.

**Fort St-Louis** Located within the Kahnawake Mohawk Territory, the Caughnawaga Mission/Mission of St. Francis Xavier National Historic Site of Canada and the

Caughnawaga Presbytery National Historic Site are located in the northeast section of the fort.

**Fort Stanwix** British fort, Rome, NY, built 1758–1762. In 1768 the Fort Stanwix Treaty conference, arranged by Johnson, took place here between the British and Iroquois. Renamed Fort Schuyler during the American Revolution, when it withstood a siege by the British. It was reconstructed in 1974–1978 by the National Park Service.

**Fort Ticonderoga** Built as Fort Carillon by the French in 1755, following Baron Dieskau's defeat by William Johnson at Lake George. Johnson was aided by Mohawks under King Hendrick who was killed. Carillon was Montcalm's base for his attack on Fort William Henry in 1757, but it was eventually captured by Amherst in 1759 and renamed Fort Ticonderoga. It exchanged hands during the Revolution and was abandoned in 1781. It was restored in the early 20th century.

**Fort William Henry** British fort on Lake George, NY. Built in 1755, it was burned down by French in 1757 after a successful siege. A replica was reconstructed in the 1950s.


**Geneseo or Little Beard's Town** A Seneca village on the Genesee River, NY.
**Grandachiragon** A Seneca village near Honeoye Falls, NY. It was destroyed in 1687 by Denonville's expedition.
**Grand Cache** Residence of some descendants of Iroquois fur traders in Alberta.
**Grand River** The Six Nations Reserve, Ontario, is just over 73 sq. miles in area and has the largest registered Indian population in Canada. Much of the original near 1,500 sq mile territory was sold off to speculators by Joseph Brant in the late 18th century.

**Above:** Fort Ticonderoga.

**Top and Above:** Johnson Hall and the southwest stone blockhouse, one of two built as defense against attack. An early visitor to his estate wrote, "Off the river about 14 miles back, Sir William Johnson has made a new Settlement and has built a very comfortable house...At this place he is generally crowded with Indians, mostly of the 5 Nations..."

**Below:** Kahnawake in 2004.

**Honeyoe** A Seneca village in New York, it was destroyed by Sullivan's expedition in 1779.

**Iroquois Indian Museum** Situated at 324 Caverns Road, Howes Cave, NY, this museum is shaped as a longhouse to recall the traditional elm bark originals found in this area 400 years ago. As well as the museum the site has a 45-acre nature park.
**Ischua** An Iroquois village on the upper Allegheny River, NY.

**Jenuchshadego or Cornplanter's Town** On the Allegheny River, Warren County, PA, this small reservation was granted to Cornplanter in 1791, and inundated by the Kinzua Reservoir in 1965. Some 550 Seneca lost their homes to the project, and while most resettled on other Seneca lands in western New York, the Seneca considered the dam a violation of treaty rights and to this day it remains a difficulty in Seneca relations with the federal government.
**Johnson Hall** Home of Sir William Johnson 1762–1774, in present-day Johnstown, NY.

**Kahnawake** The present-day 18 sq. mile Mohawk reserve on the St. Lawrence River.
**Kanakaro or Gannagaro** An important, sizeable, Seneca village of some hundred dwellings on Boughton Hill, near Victor, NY, abandoned in the late 17th century after French attack.
**Kashong** Seneca village at Geneva, NY, destroyed by Sullivan's expedition of 1779.
**Kittanning** Mixed Delaware and Iroquois villages above Pittsburgh, PA, at the end of a trail across the Alleghenies. Attacked in a raid led by Lt.-Col. John Armstrong in 1756, when the buildings were burned.

**Lachine** An Iroquois village in the Montreal area, Quebec, around 1541.
**Lewiston** Shawnee village, later mixed Shawnee and Seneca, OH.
**Logan's Town** Seneca and Mingo village, Kenton, OH.
**Logstown** Mixed Delaware, Shawnee, and Iroquois settlement on the Ohio River, PA. Also important English trading post.
**Lower Mohawk Castle** Several Mohawk villages near Schoharie Creek, NY.

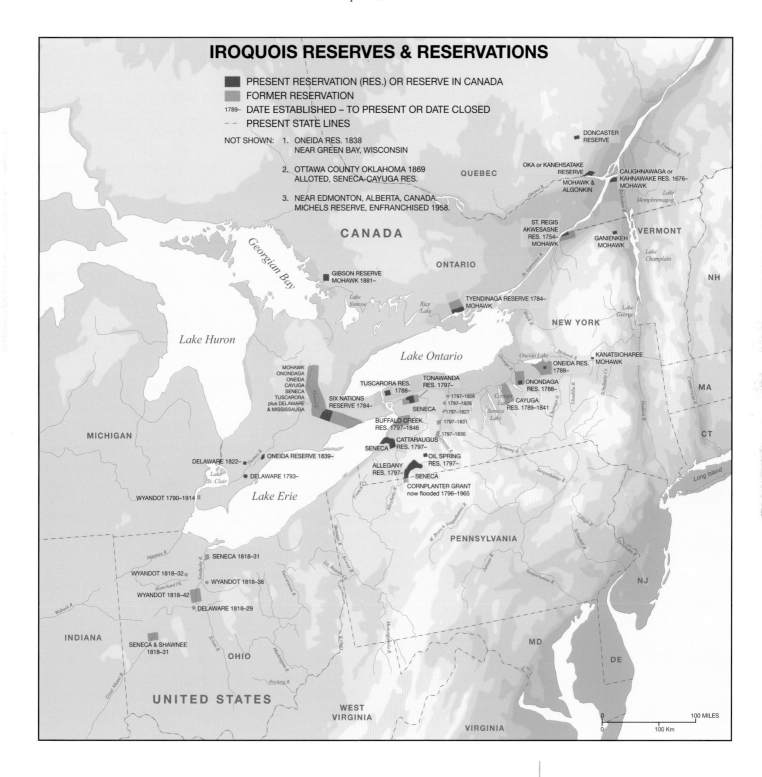

# IROQUOIS RESERVES & RESERVATIONS

■ PRESENT RESERVATION (RES.) OR RESERVE IN CANADA
■ FORMER RESERVATION
1789– DATE ESTABLISHED – TO PRESENT OR DATE CLOSED
– · – PRESENT STATE LINES
NOT SHOWN:  1. ONEIDA RES. 1838
NEAR GREEN BAY, WISCONSIN

2. OTTAWA COUNTY OKLAHOMA 1869
ALLOTED, SENECA-CAYUGA RES.

3. NEAR EDMONTON, ALBERTA, CANADA.
MICHELS RESERVE, ENFRANCHISED 1958.

**Mingo Town** Several Mingo village sites in Ohio.

**New Stockbridge** Settlement of mixed New England Algonkians near Utica, NY, in 1785; later, they moved to Wisconsin.

**Oka, Kanesatake, Lake of Two Mountains** Mixed Nipissings and Iroquois, reserve, near Montreal, Quebec.
**Oneida** Reservation in New York reduced to 32 acres by 1975 by continual sales

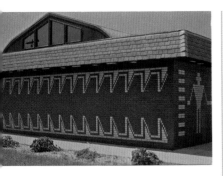

**Above:** Seneca–Iroquois National Museum, Allegany Reservation; note the exterior brickwork patterned after a wampum belt.

**Opposite, top:** Originally called St Paul's, the Mohawk Chapel is now the oldest surviving church in Ontario and the only Royal Chapel in North America. Mohawks, led by Joseph Brant, established a village here, situated at an important crossing point on the river ("Brant's Ford"). It had some 400 inhabitants by 1788. Today, only the chapel remains of the Mohawk Village. 1990 photo.

**Opposite, below left:** The tomb of Joseph Brant, Thayendanegea, and his son John, Ahyouwaighs, at the Mohawk Chapel after their remains were moved from the original burial site in Burlington, Ontario. 1990 photo.

**Below:** The Church of St. Francis-Xavier au Sault, photographed in 2004.

in Madison and Oneida counties. Turning Stone Casino has now provided wealth to repurchase land.

**Oneida of the Thames** Oneida settlement and present-day reserve, Ontario.

**Onondaga** Village of the Onondaga and capital of the league that moved location 1600–1720, ending up at Onondaga Creek, which was razed by the Continental Army in 1779. Today, the Onondaga capital is on the 9.3 sq. miles Onondaga Reservation, Onondaga County, NY. **Ossewingo** A mixed Indian village near Chenango, NY.

**Oswegatchie** A mixed Iroquois mission village in 1749, near Ogdensburgh, NY.

**Otsiningo** A mixed Iroquois, Nankicoke, Conoy, Mahican, and Shawnee village, near present-day Binghamton, NY.

**Oswego** Indian village then Fort Ontario, Oswego, NY.

**Painted Post or Assinisink** Village at or near Painted Post, NY.

**Schenectady** Town in the Mohawk Valley, NY.

**Schoharie** A mixed Mohawk and Mahican village, Schoharie Creek, NY.

**Seneca of Sandusky** Seneca and others in a reservation community on the Sandusky River, OH, 1818–1831, ultimately moved to Oklahoma.

**Seneca–Iroquois National Museum** Allegany Indian Reservation, Salamanca, NY.

**Shamokin** Indian village of mixed Delawares, Shawnees, and Iroquois at the junction of the north and west branches of the Susquehanna River, Sunbury, PA. Became Fort Augusta built in 1756.

**Six Nations Reserve** Large Iroquois settlement from 1784 of all Iroquois tribes plus Delawares and Mississaugas on a land grant made available to Iroquois following British defeat in the American Revolution, in Ontario, Upper Canada, also called Grand River Reserve.

**Squakie Hill** Village on the Genesee River, NY, named after some Mesquakies settled there after fighting the French in the 18th century (1712 on).

**St. Francis-Xavier au Sault** Church at the Indian reserve of Caughnawaga (Kahnawake), Quebec, Canada. Here lie the remains of Kateri Tekakwitha (The Lily of the Mohawks), died 1680.

**St. Paul's Chapel of the Mohawks** Built with grant obtained by Joseph Brant from George III in 1785, it was the first Protestant Church in Ontario. Today it is in Six Nations Reserve, Ontario.

**Tioga** A village of mixed Iroquois, Saponis, Tutelos, Nanticokes, Munsees, and Mahicans on the Susquehanna River at its junction with the Chemung.

**Tonawanda** Seneca village and present-day Tonawanda Reservation, Lewiston, N.Y.

**Tuscarora** Tuscarora settlement and current Tuscarora Reservation, Lewiston, N.Y.

**Upper Mohawk Castle** The most westerly part of Canajoharie, in Herkimer County, NY. Today designated an Historic District, it contains Indian Castle Church, a missionary church built in 1769 on the orders of Sir William Johnson.

**Upper Sandusky** A mixed Wyandot and Mingo village on the Sandusky River, OH.

**Venango** A Delaware village in 1740s and 1750s; later inhabited by Senecas, Shawnees, Wyandots, and Ottawas under French control (Fort Venango), near Franklin, PA.

**Wyalusing** A Munsee and Iroquois village and Moravian Mission 1763–1772, near present-day town of same name in Pennslyvania.

**Wyoming** A mixed Indian village of Munsees, Delawares, Iroquois, and Mahicans near present-day Wilkes-Barre, PA.

**Below:** One of the stained-glass windows at the Mohawk Chapel, depicting Joseph Brant receiving Rev. John Stuart on the banks of the Grand River where the church was built in 1785.

# Appendices

## 1 COMMON PRESENT-DAY IROQUOIS SURNAMES

**Six Nations, Grand River, Ontario**
Atkins, Beaver, Brant, Bomberry, Doxtater, Jamieson, Johnson, Jones, King, Hill, Montour, Maracle, Powless, Porter, Smith, Stonefish, Skye

**Akwesasne, St. Regis Reservation, NY/Ontario and Quebec**
Arquette, Chubb, Cook, Francis, George, Gray, Herne, Jacobs, Jock, King, Lazore, Martin, McDonald, Mitchell, Oakes, Pappineau, Peters, Thomas, Tarbell, White

**Allegany Reservation, NY**
Abrams, Barnwell, Bowen, Cooper, Crouse, Fatty, George, Gordon, Hill, Jimerson, John, Johnson, Kenjockety, Kettle, Kennedy, Lee, Oldshield, Pierce, Printup, Redeye, Shongo, Snow, Watt

**Caughnawaga Reserve, Quebec**
Canadian, Cross, Curotte, Deer, Diabo, Goodleaf, Horn, Jacobs, Johnson, McComber, Montour, Norton, Phillips, Rice

**Cattaraugus Reservation, NY**
Bennett, Blueskye, Button, Conklin, Doxtator, Gordon, Green, Huff, Jimerson, John, Kennedy, Kettle, Logan, Maybee, Parker, Redeye, Seneca, Snow, Tallchief, Thompson, White

**Gibson, Watha Reserve, Ontario**
Commandant, Decaire, Sahanatien, Stock

**Oka or Lake of Two Mountains Reserve, Quebec**
Babtiste, Cree, Gaspe, Laforce, Simon

**Onondaga Reservation, NY**
Diabo, George, Gibson, Hill, Jones, Johnson, La Forte, Lyons, Nolan, Pierce, Powless, Printup, Schenandoah, Skenandoah, Smoke, Stout, Thomas, Waterman

**Oneida of the Thames Reserve, Ontario**
Antone, Chrisjohn, Cornelius, Dockstader, Doxtator, Day, French, George, Henry, Ireland, Jewell, Nicholas, Powless, Snake, Sickles

**Oneida Reservation, NY**
Halbritter, Skenandoah

**Oneida Reservation, WI**
Archiquette, Cornelius, Dacotau, Doxtator, King, Metoxden, Skenandore, Powless, Smith, Stevens, Swamp, Wheelock

**Pauls Band, Michel's Reserve, Alberta**
Calihoo, Potts, Rabbit

**Seneca–Cayuga, OK**
Armstrong, Charloe, Crow, Gourd, Jamison, Logan, Mingo, Moore, Nuckolls, Perryman, Smith, Spicer, Wabaunsee, Whitetree, Wuckolls, Young

**Tonawanda Reservation, NY**
Abrams, Black, Blueye, Clute, Doctor, George, Ground, Hill, Logan, Moses, Parker, Peters, Poodry, Scrogg, Sundown, Tahamont, Tallchief

**Tuscarora Reservation, NY**
Anderson, Bissell, Chew, Gansworth, Greene, Hewitt, Hill, Jacob, Jones, Johnson, Mt. Pleasant, Patterson, Printup, Seeloff, Wilson, Zomont

**Tyendinaga Reserve, Ontario**
Barnhardt, Brant, Claus, Green, Hill, Maracle, Martin, Moses, Sero, Walker, Zachariah

## 2 IROQUOIS RESERVES, RESERVATIONS, AND POPULATIONS

Reserves, reservations, communities and populations enrolled in the US, registered in Canada.

| Tribe/Nation | Reserve/ Reservation | State/ Province | 1949 | 1970 | 1972/ 1973 | 2001 BIA | 2005 INAC |
|---|---|---|---|---|---|---|---|
| Cayuga Nation | Cattaraugus and others | NY | 200 | | | 474 | |
| Oneida Nation | Oneida and Onondaga Reservations | NY | 350 | | | 1,893 | |
| Onondaga Nation | Onondaga Reservation | NY | 1,000 | | | NR 1 | |
| Seneca Nation | Allegany and Cattaraugus Reservations | NY | | | | 7,118 | |
| Seneca | Allegany Reservation alone | NY | 1,000 | | | — | |
| Seneca | Cattaraugus Reservation alone | NY | 2,000 | | | — | |
| Seneca | Tonawanda Band, Tonawanda Reservation | NY | 600 | | | NR 2 | |
| Tuscarora Nation | Tuscarora Reservation | NY | 450 | | | NR 3 | |
| Akwesasne Mohawks | St. Regis Reservation | NY | 1,800 | | | 9,020 | |
| Mohawks of Akwesasne | St. Regis Reservation | Ontario Quebec | 609 1,171 | ) ) 2,963 | | | 10,217 |
| Mohawks of Kahnawake | Caughnawaga Reserve | Quebec | 3,198 | 4,515 | | | 9,392 |
| Mohawks of Kanesatake | Oka or Lake of Two Mountains Reserve | Quebec | 507 | 777 | | | 2,017 |
| Mohawks of the Bay of Quinte | Tyendinaga Reserve | Ontario | 1,601 | 2,111 | | | 7,533 +637 |
| Watha Mohawks | Gibson Reserve | Ontario | 241 | 206 | | | 671 |
| Lower Mohawks | Six Nations Reserve | Ontario | ) | ) | ) | | 3,542 |
| Upper Mohawks | Six Nations Reserve | Ontario | ) | ) | ) 3,974 | | 5,264 +431 |
| Lower Cayuga | Six Nations Reserve | Ontario | ) | ) | ) | | 3,105 |
| Upper Cayuga | Six Nations Reserve | Ontario | )6,003 | )8,680 | ) 2,525 | | 3,042 |
| Oneida | Six Nations Reserve | Ontario | ) | ) | 802 | | 1,784 |
| Onondaga | Six Nations Reserve | Ontario | ) | ) | 560 | | 662 |
| Seneca | Six Nations Reserve | Ontario | ) | ) | 345 | | 487 +349 |
| Tuscarora | Six Nations Reserve | Ontario | ) | ) | 789 | | 1,926 |
| Oneida Nation of the Thames | Oneidatown Reserve | Ontario | 1,068 | 2,011 | 1,964 | | 5,127 |
| Oneida | Oneida Reservation | WI | | | 6,684 | 14,745 | |
| Seneca–Cayuga | Former Seneca–Cayuga Reservation | OK | 900 | | | 3,674 | |
| Iroquois | Michel's Reserve | Alberta | 123 Enfranchised 1958 | | | | |
| Mohawk | Ganienkeh | NY | | NFR | | | |
| Mohawk | Kanatsioharee | NY | | NFR | | | |

NR = not reported: **1** c. 2,000; **2** c. 1,000; **3** c. 1,000

INAC = Indian & Northern Affairs Canada

BIA = Bureau of Indian Affairs, US Dept. of the Interior

NFR = Not federally recognized     + = more than

| | US | CANADA |
|---|---|---|
| TOTAL | 40,924 | 56,186 |
| GRAND TOTAL | 97,110 | |

# Bibliography

Bicheno, Hugh: *Rebels & Redcoats The American Revolutionary War*; Harper Collins, London, UK, 2003.

Biron, Gerry: *A Cherished Curiosity, The Souvenir Beaded Bag in Historic Haudenosaunee (Iroquois) Art*; self-published, Saxtons, River, VT, 2012.

Diefendorf, Mary Briggs: *The Historic Mohawk*; G.P. Putman & Sons, New York, NY, 1910.

Ewers, John C.: *Gustavus Sohon's portraits of Flathead and Pend d'Oreille Indians 1854*; Smithsonian Institution, Washington, DC, 1948.

Fenton, William N.: *Tonawanda Longhouse Ceremonies Ninety Years after Lewis Henry Morgan*; Anthropological Papers, No. 15, Bulletin 128, Smithsonian Institution, Washington, DC, 1941.

--------*The False Faces of the Iroquois*; University of Oklahoma Press, Norman, OK, 1987.

Holler, Deborah: "The Remarkable Caroline G. Parker Mountpleasant Seneca Wolf Clan"; *Western New York Heritage Magazine*, Vol. 14, No. 1, Western New York Heritage Press, Cheektowaga, NY, 2011.

Jennings, Francis (ed.): *The History and Culture of Iroquois Diplomacy*; Syracuse University Press, Syracuse, NY, 1985.

Johnson, Michael, and Hook, Richard: *Encyclopaedia of Native American Tribes*, third edition; Compendium Publishing Ltd., London, UK, 2007.

Johnson, Michael, and Smith, Jonathan: *Tribes of the Iroquois Confederacy*; Osprey Publishing Ltd., Oxford, UK, 2003.

Kelsay, Isabel Thompson: *Joseph Brant 1743–1807 Man of Two Worlds*; Syracuse University Press, Syracuse, NY, 1984.

King, J.C.H.: *Thunderbird and Lightning, Indian Life in Northeastern North America 1600–1900*; British Museum Publications Ltd., London, UK, 1982.

Kurath, Gertrude P.: *Iroquois Music and Dance, Ceremonial Arts of two Seneca Longhouses*; Bureau of American Ethnology, Bulletin 187, Smithsonian Institution, Washington, DC, 1964.

--------*Dance and Song Rituals of Six Nations Reserve, Ontario*; National Museum of Canada, Bulletin No. 220, Folklore Series No. 4, Ottawa, Canada, 1968.

Lydekker, John Wolfe: *The Faithful Mohawks*; Cambridge University Press, Cambridge, UK, 1938.

Lyford, Carrie A.: *Iroquois Crafts*; Indian Handicraft Pamphlet No. 6, Haskell Institute, Lawrence, KS, 1945.

--------*Iroquois Their Art and Crafts*; Hancock House Publishers Ltd., Surrey, BC, Canada, 1989.

McKenney, Thomas L., and Hall, James (ed. F.W. Hodge): *The Indian Tribes of North America*; three volumes; John Grant, Edinburgh, UK 1933–34.

Morgan, Lewis H.: *League of the Ho-de-no-sau-nee, or Iroquois*; two volumes; Dodd, Mead & Co., New York, NY, 1851.

--------*Report to the Regents of the University (of the State of New York) upon the Articles Furnished to the Indian Collection*; 1849. Reprinted in Tooker, 1994.

--------*Report on the Fabrics, Inventions, Implements and Utensils of the Iroquois, made to the Regents of the University (of the State of New York)*; 1851. Reprinted in Tooker, 1994.

O'Toole, Fintan: *White Savage William Johnson and the Invention of America*; Faber & Faber Ltd., London, UK, 2005.

Speck, Frank G.: *The Iroquois A Study in Cultural Evolution*; Cranbrook Institute of Science, Bulletin No. 23; Bloomfield Hills, MI, 1945.

Sturtevant, William C. (gen. ed.) and Trigger, Bruce G. (ed.): *Handbook of North American Indians, Vol. 15 Northeast*; Smithsonian Institution, Washington, DC, 1978.

Tanner, Helen Hornbeck (ed.): *Atlas of Great Lakes Indian History*; University of Oklahoma Press, Norman, OK, 1987.

Tooker, Elizabeth: *Lewis H. Morgan on Iroquois Material Culture*; The University of Arizona Press, 1994.

Wallace, Paul A.W.: *Indians in Pennsylvania*; The Pennsylvania Historical and Museum Commission, Harrisburg, PA, 1961.

# Index